THE ART OF THE
SANDWICH

by Jay Harlow

PHOTOGRAPHY BY
Viktor Budnik

Food Styling by
Diane Elander

CHRONICLE BOOKS · SAN FRANCISCO

This book is dedicated to Dick Schuettge,
with thanks for years of generosity and patient advice.

LIBRARY OF CONGRESS CATALOGING-IN-PUBLICATION DATA

Harlow, Jay, 1953–
    The art of the sandwich / by Jay Harlow ; photography by Viktor
Budnik.
        p.   cm.
    ISBN 0-87701-748-4
    1. Sandwiches. I. Title.
TX818.H356 1990
641.8′4—dc20   90–32147
                                                      CIP

Editing: Elaine Ratner
Design: Paula Schlosser Design
Typography: Classic Typography, Ukiah, CA
Produced by Astolat Productions
Printed in Japan

Distributed in Canada by Raincoast Books
112 East 3rd Avenue
Vancouver, B.C., V5T 1C8

10 9 8 7 6 5 4 3 2 1

Chronicle Books
275 Fifth Street
San Francisco, California 94103

CONTENTS

Acknowledgments

The author would like to thank the following people and organizations for their help in producing this book:

Viktor Budnik and Diane Elander, for truly representing the "art" of the sandwich.

Pam Palmer, Karen Lucas, Lisa Wilson, and Wendy Hallinan for generously contributing recipes. Jim Dodge, for his constant and cheerful willingness to advise me on baking techniques, as well as for his ideas on tea sandwiches. Kim Davenport, Eddie Orton, and Amy Silver for taking Rebecca on all-day outings, so Daddy and Mommy could work all weekend and get the manuscript in on time.

Jillann Wood, for help in gathering props for photography; B.G. Ferguson of Oakland, Fillamento of San Francisco, and TzinTzunTzan Warehouse of Berkeley, for their beautiful plates and other props.

Eddie Orton, Adam Levine, and the Vulcan Cafe in Oakland; Ronnie White of Kilpatrick's Bakeries, Inc., Oakland; Roberta Klugman, San Francisco International Cheese Imports; P.G. Molinari & Sons, San Francisco.

At Chronicle Books, Jack Jensen, Nion McEvoy, Julie Noyes, Karen Pike, Bill LeBlond, and Mary Ann Gilderbloom. Deborah Stone and Carey Charlesworth, for their editorial help.

Paula Schlosser, for her excellent eye and fine design. Stan Shoptaugh of Classic Typography, for another fine job of typesetting.

And, as always, to Elaine Ratner, partner, editor, wife, and mother par excellence. I always thought "better half" was a corny expression, but she truly brings out the best I have to offer, and then makes it better.

INTRODUCTION

I REMEMBER A JOKE from many years ago: A couple of working men are opening up their lunch pails when one moans, "Cheese sandwich again. Every day a cheese sandwich."

"Why don't you ask your wife to make you something different?" asks the other.

"Whaddya mean my wife? I make my own lunch!"

Sandwiches are so much a part of our everyday lives, it is easy to take them for granted. It's also easy to get into a rut, making the same old combinations day in and day out.

When you expand your sandwich thinking beyond meat and cheese between two slices of bread, a whole new world of possibilities opens up. Why not build a sandwich around a pancake of grated zucchini and eggs? Or some slices of Chinese-style roast duck? Or grilled eggplant? If you can put vegetables in sandwiches, why not fruit?

A good sandwich begins with good bread. Living in and around Berkeley, California for the last few years, I have been happy witness to a bread renaissance. A handful of small bakeries has totally transformed the local bread market in the last decade, producing an ever-growing variety of flavorful breads both rustic and refined. Even the supermarkets are stocking a wider variety of breads than ever before. I hear the same from other parts of the country, where good honest bread is making a comeback after years of sliced balloon bread.

With all this good bread around, a lot of it is being put to use by creative sandwich makers. In fact, one of my favorite restaurants now in Berkeley is a sandwich shop. At Panini, owner Lee Ann Sandefer makes an assortment of delicious Italian-inspired sandwiches, each of which is a carefully thought-out combination of a particular bread, filling, and garnish. It was at one of my lunches there that I began thinking about how satisfying a great sandwich can be, and the idea of a sandwich cookbook was born.

Although the recipes in this book are for my favorite sandwiches, the glossary of sandwich ingredients in the first chapter covers the basic building blocks of any good sandwich. I hope it will help you to create your own combinations.

A simple ham and cheese on rye can be a memorable lunch, as long as it's made with good ham, good cheese, and good rye. Just remember that sandwiches, like anything you cook, deserve to be made with the best ingredients. And remember that sandwiches are casual, light-hearted foods, so experiment with new combinations and have fun.

Jay Harlow
Berkeley, California

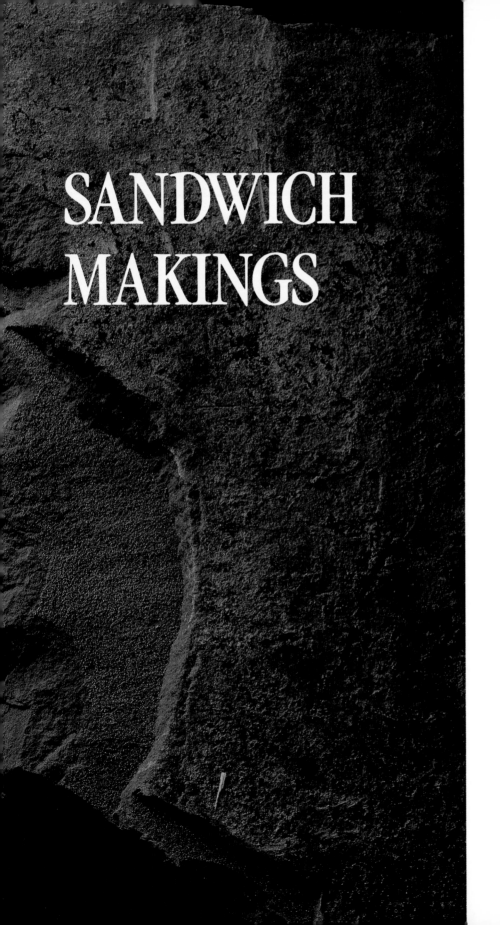

SANDWICH MAKINGS

The Art of Creative Sandwich Making

There are no secrets to making great sandwiches. The same principles that are fundamental to all good food apply as well to a good sandwich: Use good ingredients. Combine them with care, and with an eye to variety and balance of flavors and textures. And present the finished product attractively.

In a good sandwich, all the elements—the bread, filling, spread, and garnish—work together to create a harmonious effect. Sometimes one element is the star and the others play supporting roles; at other times it's the combination of many characters that makes a satisfying whole.

First, consider the flavors you are combining. It may help to think in terms of the system of five flavors identified by the Chinese several thousand years ago—sweet, sour, salty, bitter, and pungent (hot). Not all of these flavors have to be present in every dish or even every meal, but they should be used as elements of balance and contrast. You wouldn't want to make a sandwich entirely of salty foods, or use all sour or sweet flavors.

Consider also the intensity of the flavors you use. It takes only a little bit of a highly flavored ingredient such as anchovy to accent the sweet, earthy onion flavor of braised leeks. A small amount of chile-flavored salsa is plenty to season a burrito or quesadilla. At the other extreme, think of bland foods such as mild cheeses, beans, and most breads to serve as background for stronger flavors.

Let's look at one recipe, the Dried Tomato, Cream Cheese, and Arugula Sandwich on page 23, to see how these principles work. The sun-dried tomatoes concentrate the sweet and acid flavor of ripe summer tomatoes, and they also contain some salt (both natural and added). By themselves, they are too intense to be used in quantity. But by chopping them and mixing them with bland cream cheese, you can spread their flavor throughout a sandwich. By itself, this combination is still a bit simple; a little bit of bitter, peppery arugula adds just the accent needed. Replace the cream cheese with a tangy goat cheese (as I did when testing the recipe) and you destroy the balance; the sharp, sour flavor of the cheese and tomatoes combined is too much. An especially sour bread would have the same effect.

Texture is another essential but sometimes overlooked quality of foods. Chewy or tender, crunchy or smooth, dry or moist—these qualities are as much a part of the overall impression of the food as the flavor. One of the main reasons people put lettuce in sandwiches is to provide a bit of crunch among the softer textures of the bread and filling. Of course, the bread itself can provide plenty of texture; think of sandwiches on crusty French rolls or dense pumpernickel. The key is to match the bread with the filling. The bread should not be so much harder than the filling that everything squeezes out when you take a bite, nor should it be so soft that it collapses or comes apart against a firm-textured filling.

There are times when the form of the sandwich dictates a uniform texture, as in the Turkey and Cranberry Roll on page 66. Everything in this sandwich is necessarily soft, so serve it with a good crunchy pickle or other garnish to satisfy your need for chewier stuff.

The Creative Process

The recipes in this book are examples of successful combinations of flavors and textures. Use them as a guide to unleash your own creativity. Think of food combinations that you have enjoyed and consider how they might be adapted to a sandwich. That's how I came up with a sandwich of blue cheese and pears on walnut bread. A Greek salad I enjoyed in Athens became the stuffed pita sandwich on page 69. A chef I know makes a version of Carnitas (see page 77) with duck in place of pork.

If you get stuck, or need ideas for something to combine with an ingredient, do what my friend Jim Dodge, a great pastry chef, does: Taste the two items together. Take a bite of X, then a bite of Y, and see if the flavors complement each other. Maybe Y doesn't work, but it suggests another flavor, so try that combination. A bit of tasting beforehand might save you from a disappointing sandwich or steer you toward a better one.

Of course, it helps to have a variety of ingredients on hand to inspire you. Keep the basics—mustards, mayonnaise, assorted breads, greens, herbs—in your pantry and refrigerator, and always be on the lookout for canned, bottled, dried, or otherwise durable ingredients that can give a new twist to an old favorite.

A Sandwich Maker's Glossary

The following is a catalog of selected sandwich makings. It offers advice on selecting, storing, and using many of the ingredients called for in the recipes in this book. Also included are a number of ingredients not used in the recipes but useful in sandwich making. Browse through the section for ideas to guide you and inspire your own sandwich creativity.

BREAD

Although every sandwich begins with bread, not every sandwich maker takes bread as seriously as it deserves. No matter how fine the filling, a sandwich cannot reach its highest potential on an inferior or inappropriate slice of bread. An excellent piece of bread, on the other hand, can become a satisfying sandwich with the simple addition of a slice of good cheese.

Sliced Bread

Americans love innovation and convenience, and so they fell in love with sliced bread when it was introduced in the 1920s. It has become a part of all of our lives, as has the expression "the greatest thing since sliced bread." But what's so great about presliced bread? Too often it is like foam, lacking in flavor, texture, and nutrition.

Fortunately, the typical supermarket's bread selection is expanding. When I was a child, the only choices were puffy white bread, a slightly more substantial "wheat" or cracked wheat variation, rye, and perhaps a pumpernickel. Today many markets offer a wide variety of packaged whole-grain and mixed-grain breads. Unfortunately, the majority of these "healthier" breads are oversweetened. Read the ingredient lists and in addition to (or sometimes in place of) sugar you'll find corn syrup, malt syrup, raisin syrup, honey, molasses, or other sweeteners. The higher the sweeteners come in the ingredient list, the sweeter the bread will taste.

Still, the situation is improving. You can find good bread if you shop carefully. Search out the good bread bakeries in your area, and encourage grocers to stock better breads. If you have the time, it's tremendously satisfying to bake your own.

Whether you make it or shop around for it, good honest bread is worth the effort.

Loaves for Slicing

Presliced bread may be convenient, but whole loaves keep fresh longer, and allow you to cut slices the thickness you like them. In my experience, the breads sold as unsliced loaves are usually of better quality.

White Bread Many of the recipes in this book call for crusty white bread. That means a free-standing loaf (not baked in a pan) with a substantial crust and an inside with some character. Depending on where you live, this kind of bread may be called French, Italian, or Vienna bread, or something else. It is one of the most versatile sandwich breads.

It may be available in supermarkets or only through a few bakeries. It may come in various "flavors," including sourdough and sweet. It may come already sliced, but the unsliced version is usually crustier. If you can't find a basic crusty white loaf to your liking, try the recipe for Pane all'Olio on page 86.

Whole Wheat Bread Breads made from whole grains are nutritionally superior to white breads, because much of the vitamin and fiber content is removed from white flour before it is ground. Whole grain breads also taste better and have more interesting textures. I use whole wheat bread for sandwiches unless there is a good reason not to—if the texture of the filling requires a crusty roll to contain it, for instance, or when a hearty-flavored bread would overwhelm a delicately flavored filling. A recipe for an all-purpose, everyday whole wheat bread appears on page 85.

Rye Bread Rye bread, which is stronger tasting than both white and whole wheat bread, is another sandwich maker's staple. Because rye flour does not contain as much gluten as wheat flour, it tends to make a heavier bread. Most rye breads have white flour added to make a lighter loaf. Two exceptions, pumpernickel and *schwarzbröt,* are dense, moist all-rye breads.

I think supermarket rye bread tends to be better than most other types of supermarket bread. The basic choice is between loaves with and without caraway seeds. Loaves rolled in cornmeal before baking are labeled "corn rye" or sometimes "New York style." Dark rye is not necessarily any stronger in flavor than light rye; it is colored with dark molasses or dark malt syrup, to give it a traditional appearance. The heartiest rye breads I have found are the large loaves (or sections of even larger loaves) sold unsliced in some delicatessens and bakeries.

Rolls and Baguettes

Some sandwiches just don't seem right on anything but a roll or bun. You can put a hamburger between slices of rye, or split a hot dog and serve it on French bread, but it isn't the same.

In general, the filling will determine the best roll for any given sandwich. A soft, moist filling such as lobster salad calls for a tender roll (see Maine Lobster Roll, page 24); put the same filling on a baguette and it will squoosh out as you bite through the bread. Thinly sliced meats go best on sturdier rolls or baguettes.

Sandwich Rolls Sandwich rolls come in all sizes, shapes, and textures, from soft white hamburger buns to the crustiest baguettes. Each is ideal for some sort of sandwich. *Note:* Croissants are not sandwich rolls. If you wouldn't serve ham and cheese on Danish pastry or on a muffin, don't serve it on a croissant.

Rolls vary widely in both texture and flavor. The softest include round hamburger buns, hog dog buns, and slightly wider, sometimes seeded steak rolls. Delicatessen onion rolls and sesame-topped egg rolls offer a couple of flavor options. One step up in firmness are oblong sandwich or French rolls, which may have a soft or crisp crust, and round Kaiser rolls. Any of these are good for sandwiches of sliced meats and cheeses, sausages, and hamburgers. When the rolls will be stuffed with a lot of filling, you might want to hollow them out a bit.

French Loaves and Baguettes Long French loaves cut into sections sometimes taste better than prepackaged rolls. They may be crisp or soft, sourdough or "sweet," depending on local tradition. When you want your bread really crusty, maximize the surface-to-volume ratio by using a baguette, a long, slender French loaf usually about a half pound in weight.

Quick Breads

These are raised by the chemical action of baking powder or baking soda rather than yeast. They are generally more tender and crumbly than yeast breads, and so are less useful in sandwich making. They are best for tea sandwiches, which, being small, don't need to be as sturdy as most sandwiches. If you want to use quick breads for other than tea sandwiches, remember that smaller pieces are easier to handle than full slices. The Quick Nut Bread on page 90 is a basic, versatile quick bread.

Flat Breads

Long before bread was baked in pans or even in raised loaves, the people of the eastern Mediterranean region were baking flat breads directly on stone hearths or the floors of brick ovens. This archetypal bread survives in the form of pita, the hollow round "pocket bread" of the Middle East. Other still-popular forms of flat bread include Italian pizza and focaccia, Armenian lavash, Scandinavian crispbreads, and Mexican tortillas.

Pita Pita comes in both white and whole wheat versions. As the flat bread bakes, it puffs up, forming a pocket that is perfect for stuffing. You simply slice off the top for one deep pocket or cut the pita into two equal halves for two smaller pockets. The typical pita is 6 inches in diameter, but some bakeries make a smaller snack size. Although I like the flavor of the whole wheat variety, I find white-flour pitas a little easier to handle. Stuffed pita sandwiches are on pages 67-71, and a recipe for baking your own pitas is on page 93.

Lavash Wherever Armenian immigrants have settled in numbers, notably around Fresno, California and in parts of Massachusetts, there are bakeries producing the crackerlike lavash. (*Lavasch, lahvosh* and other spellings are also used—each bakery seems to have made its own transliteration a trademark.) Some lavash are small and rectangular, but the widely distributed version from the Valley Bakery of Fresno is in large round sheets, packed three to a one-pound bag. This is the type which, when softened with water, can be rolled around a stuffing to make a pinwheel-shaped sandwich (see pages 64-66). A recipe for homemade lavash appears on page 92.

Crispbread The Scandinavian countries are home to many flat breads, most made partly or entirely of rye flour. Dry, they can be a base for *smørrebrød* (see page 58); larger sheets can be softened and used for rolled sandwiches just like lavash.

Tortillas, unleavened round cornmeal breads baked on a hot stone, were the bread staple of pre-Columbian Mexico and Central America, and remain an essential food today. After the Spanish introduced both wheat and pigs, white flour tortillas made with lard became the dominant bread in the northern states of Mexico.

Both flour and corn tortillas are widely available in North American markets now, although brands vary widely in quality. Flour tortillas range in size from 6-inch fajita size to 14-inch or larger super burrito size. The flour tortillas I prefer for quesadillas and burritos are called *gorditas* and are a little thicker than usual (the label says "like handmade"); they also happen to be made with vegetable shortening rather than lard.

Focaccia This flat Italian bread, a cousin of pizza, is a yeast-raised bread, an inch or more thick and very rich with olive oil. It's sold in Italian bakeries and delis by the whole or half sheet or cut into squares. Split and filled with a thin layer of meat or cheese, it makes an elegant and very Italian sandwich (see page 27).

Focaccia often comes topped with an herb (frequently rosemary); there are also more complicated toppings, including tomatoes, olives, or cheese. Use the plainest version you can find for sandwiches. The related French *fougasse* is denser, with a heavier crust, and is often formed into a leaf shape; it is less suitable for sandwiches.

MEAT

Just about any cooked meat that can be sliced is a potential sandwich filling. One trip to a good delicatessen can easily give you a week's worth of inspiration. Here are some tips on the most popular sandwich meats.

Ham

Most delis carry at least two varieties of ham, one "boiled" and one baked or smoked. A well-stocked counter may carry eight to ten varieties of ham, each cured or shaped in a distinctive way and having a particular flavor.

Although ham is commonly thought of as smoked pork, by no means all hams are smoked. The basic treatment that turns fresh pork into ham is a preserving cure of salt, which draws excess moisture out of the meat. Some of the salt soaks

into the meat during the curing process, and the combination of lower moisture and high salt concentration prevents bacteria or parasites from spoiling the meat. Other treatments, including added ingredients in the cure, smoking, and air-drying, determine the flavor and texture of the final product.

Pale pink, lightly cured boiled and canned hams are typically the least expensive and the mildest; their flavor is dominated by salt and perhaps sugar. Slightly darker and drier, and usually more flavorful, are smoked and baked hams. These are typically round or oval, and may show marks from the netting in which they were hung during curing or smoking. Strongly smoked and very flavorful, but still on the moist side, is Black Forest-style ham, one of my favorites for sandwiches.

Dry-cured hams, including Italian prosciutto, German Westphalian ham, and Spanish Serrano ham, go through a heavier cure and a long dry-aging process which produce deeply colored, dense-textured hams for slicing very thin. For years, U.S. regulations kept many of the traditional European dry-cured hams out of this country, limiting us to locally made versions, many of which are excellent. Our choices became wider beginning in the late 1980s, when USDA-inspected European plants began to ship some of their classic products in newly approved form. Although these specialty hams, imported or domestic, are expensive, a little goes a long way; a couple of ounces of prosciutto deliver as much flavor as a quarter pound or more of a milder ham. Use them when they can really shine, as in the Prosciutto and Artichoke Sandwich pictured on the cover (recipe, page 27).

Other Cured Meats

Cured beef in various forms is another staple of the deli counter. A few of the most popular forms are listed here.

Corned beef, beef brisket cured in a spiced brine, is a perennial sandwich favorite. You can buy ready-to-cook corned brisket and cook it yourself, or buy it already cooked at the deli.

Pickled tongue is beef tongue treated the same way as corned beef. You may also find it smoked.

Pastrami is cured like corned beef, though with a different blend of spices; then it is smoked, giving it a firmer texture and stronger flavor. Beef plate, the cut just behind the brisket, is traditionally used for Eastern-style pastrami, but brisket is also common. Western packers often use round, either a well-marbled bottom round or the leaner eye of round and top round. These cuts are frequently labeled "pepper beef" to distinguish them from the fattier plate or brisket varieties. If you plan to serve pastrami hot, choose plate or brisket for a moist, juicy result; if you are making a cold sandwich, use a leaner type.

Roast Beef

Most deli versions are from the round, but sliced leftovers of any tender roast make a good sandwich. Roast beef should still be pink in the middle; any cooked beyond medium rare is likely to be too dry when sliced thin.

Salami

Like ham, salami covers a wide range of products. Most are ready-to-eat sausages of coarsely ground meat (pork, beef, or a blend) in which flecks of fat are visible. Dry (Italian) salami is the densest form; as it ages it shrinks into a firm cylinder that can be stored at room temperature and sliced very thinly. Different salami recipes may be identified with individual Italian cities or regions (Genovese, Toscana, Calabrese) but they are interchangeable in use.

Coppa is not strictly a salami; it is pork shoulder cured like prosciutto, then formed into a cylinder and aged like salami. It may be mild or hot.

Other forms of salami are larger in diameter and moister than Italian, and need to be refrigerated. These include kosher salami (which contains no pork, of course) and Italian *cotto*.

Other Sausages

Also of interest to the sandwich maker are the kids' favorite, bologna, and its progenitor, mortadella. Both are finely ground, mildly seasoned, tender and moist; a mixture of pork, veal, and beef is typical. Liverwurst and Braunschweiger are soft, spreadable liver sausages; all they need is a touch of good mustard on the bread and a few lettuce leaves to make a satisfying sandwich. And then there are all those rolled or loaf-shaped preparations that reflect the creativity and thrift of the *charcutier*—head cheese, tongue loaf, pistachio loaf, and on and on.

Pâtés and Terrines

These rich mixtures of ground and cooked meats range from a coarse country-style pork and veal *pâté de campagne* (basically a French meat loaf) to silky-smooth liver pâtés. A quarter-inch slice of dense pâté on good bread with a smear of mustard is a simple but memorable sandwich. Fresh pâtés can be found in many delis. There are also some good canned versions, a nice thing to have on hand in the pantry. Strictly speaking, a pâté is baked inside a pastry crust (which is meant to be removed before eating) and any that is not is called a terrine (after the container in which it is baked); this distinction is "more honored in the breach than the observance."

Poultry

While they bring us more processed turkey products, including turkey ham, turkey bologna, and turkey pastrami, the poultry industry keeps trying to refine its most popular delicatessen product, plain cooked turkey breast. In search of a moister, more "natural"-tasting product, they now offer boneless breast halves or chunks in vacuum-sealed packages, plain or "barbe-cued." There are also packages of perfectly round, standard-size slices hanging next to the bologna and salami in the super-market refrigerator case.

Most of these newer forms of turkey breast have something wrong with them to my taste—either too much gelatinous binder or a funny-tasting broth. I prefer to stick with the turkey roll that packagers have been selling for years. By that I mean not the cylindrical version made up of both light and dark meat, but several boneless breasts formed together into a more or less natural shape, wrapped in turkey skin and cooked. As long as you have it sliced to order, keep it tightly wrapped, and use it within a day or two after you buy it, it stays moist.

Of course, if you have the time and refrigerator space, it's always best to cook your own turkey. Leftover roast turkey makes great sandwiches, and not just after Thanksgiving. Its only fault is that it can be hard to slice thinly, especially when the whole bird is roasted until the thighs are fully done. Try braising or poaching a whole or half breast instead. Cooked to an internal temperature of 160°, it will be moist and easy to slice.

Both turkey and chicken are sometimes available smoked. Try specialty poultry stores or well-stocked delicatessens (you may have to order in advance). Smoked poultry is fully cooked in the smoking process, is generally quite juicy, and will keep for several days in the refrigerator.

Seafood

Beyond the obvious canned tuna, there are a number of seafood products that make good sandwich material. Sardines and pickled herring are ideal for open-face sandwiches. (At least one herring dish is essential if you're making a spread of Danish *smørrebrød*; see page 61.) Cooked crabmeat or peeled and deveined shrimp make great sandwich fillings; mix either with mayonnaise or pureed ricotta cheese and chopped fresh dill, and pile it into a soft roll.

Smoked fish is another traditional element in *smørrebrød*. The finest cold-smoked salmon (lox) deserves the simplest treatment—a plain piece of buttered bread. (Of course, it is also sublime on a split bagel spread with cream cheese.) Hot-smoked fish, sometimes called kippered, can take stronger flavorings such as horseradish and capers. Herring, whitefish, tuna,

sturgeon, trout, Pacific sablefish (black cod), and salmon are among the hot-smoked fish suitable for *smørrebrød*.

Canned tuna has generated some controversy, because the fishing methods used to catch some varieties of tuna can kill or maim dolphins as well. Actually, this is only a problem with light tuna, specifically yellowfin tuna taken in the eastern tropical Pacific. White tuna (albacore), tongol tuna from Southeast Asia and the Indian Ocean, and bonito are all dolphin-safe. If you prefer to avoid canned tuna, you can buy fresh or frozen tuna or bonito, poach it, and moisten the cooked meat with seasoned olive oil.

Storage

Keep sliced meats refrigerated, tightly wrapped. The original butcher-paper wrapping is good for a day or so if not opened, but it's not airtight and meats may dry out slightly. For longer storage, rewrap the food in plastic wrap (see page 15).

A slight rainbow iridescence on the surface of cured meats, by the way, is not a sign of spoilage; it's a natural effect, probably caused by the way the light strikes the molecules of salt or nitrates in the cure.

CHEESE

With hundreds of varieties of cheese available, it's easy to get lost in a well-stocked cheese shop. The best approach is to learn something about each of the major cheese families. Although the individual members of each family differ somewhat, they share certain basic qualities. Once you are familiar with the attributes of a family and know you like it, you can substitute one family member for another in recipes according to what is available or your mood.

Try to buy your cheese from shops that let you sample. Similar cheeses can taste quite different, and even the same cheese will vary from brand to brand or, within a brand, from one shipment to the next.

The following is by no means a complete listing of cheese families, but rather a catalog of the types most useful in sandwich making.

Cheddar Types

Cheddar and its relatives, including Colby, Jack, and American, are the most familiar cheeses to Americans. They are descendants of the original Cheddar made in west-central England. When young, cheeses of the cheddar family are relatively soft, high in moisture, and mild; block American cheese is a good example. With age they become drier, more crumbly, and quite sharp in flavor, like the English original. Between the extremes are some of our most popular sandwich cheeses.

Domestic cheddars ranging from mild to sharp are made everywhere there is dairy farming; random-size cuts from large blocks of cheddar are found in every supermarket. Most are easily sliced, making them a good choice for sandwiches. There are several regional versions that vary significantly in flavor and texture. Excellent New York and Vermont cheddars are shipped all over the country, and Tillamook from Oregon is widely available in the West. Older Wisconsin cheddars are often too crumbly for easy slicing, as are true English Cheddar and most of its English cousins. These are best as table rather than sandwich cheeses. Orange-colored Colby and mild, white, slightly tangy Jack (sometimes called Monterey Jack) are distant relatives of cheddar and are fine for sandwiches.

Swiss Types

The original Swiss cheese, variously spelled Emmental, Emmenthal, and Emmenthaler, is one of the most imitated cheeses in the world. The real thing is made in thick wheels which may weigh up to 200 pounds each. It has an incomparable sweet-nutty taste, firm texture, and the famous holes or "eyes." Cheesemakers in other countries make similar-looking cheeses, but they never taste exactly the same. French Emmental comes closest. Emmental-type cheeses are also made in Austria and Germany, and there are derivatives in most Scandinavian countries, of which I consider the Norwegian Jarlsberg the best. American dairies produce an enormous amount of "Swiss," but I've never had a memorable one.

The other classic Swiss cheese is Gruyère, which tastes similar to Emmental but is more delicate. It has a firmer texture and few or no holes. There may be no better cheese for melting on hot open-face sandwiches; cold, the texture can be slightly grainy. The best French Gruyères, including Beaufort and Comté, are at least the equal of their Swiss counterparts.

Mild Semisoft Cheeses

This broad category includes many of Europe's most famous cheeses. They are softer—that is, have a higher moisture content—than the Swiss or Cheddar types. One of the best for sandwiches is Italian Fontina, preferably the one from the Val d'Aosta near the French border. It has an Alpine flavor reminiscent of Gruyère, but a softer, smoother texture; and it melts beautifully. Other Italian Fontina types are more properly labeled Fontal, and they can be quite good. Swedish Fontina is a good, inexpensive cheese; the Danish version is a little less successful but quite popular.

Other useful semisoft cheeses include Danish Havarti or Dofino, riddled with tiny bubbles and pleasantly mild; high-moisture Jack, a softer version of the type sold in blocks; and domestic Muenster, a mild cheese that has nothing in common with its strongly flavored French and German namesakes. All of these are good partners to sliced ham and other meats in cold sandwiches. Jack and Muenster are fine for topping hot open-face sandwiches.

Cream Cheese

Basically soured cream with the liquid drained out of it, this mild, smooth cheese acts as a binder, moistener, or stretcher of other ingredients. It's indispensable for tea sandwiches. "Natural" cream cheese, sold in large cylindrical or square loaves wrapped in plastic, has a slightly crumbly texture compared to the familiar foil-wrapped brands which have vegetable gums added for a smoother texture. Neufchâtel is a lower-fat version of cream cheese, sometimes labeled "light" cream cheese.

Other Fresh Cheeses

Ricotta is a fresh cheese like fine-curd cottage cheese, but it is made largely from whey rather than whole milk. It has a few uses in sandwiches (see Bruschetta with Peaches and Cheese, page 54, and Tea Sandwiches, pages 31-33).

Fresh goat cheese, either domestic or French, has a distinctive tangy flavor. I don't think it harmonizes very well with other sandwich ingredients, but spread on a slice of bread or a split baguette it makes a good simple sandwich.

Feta is a fresh sheep's milk cheese preserved in brine; it also has a singular flavor. It is used in only one recipe in this book (see Greek Salad Sandwich, page 69).

Spiced and Flavored Cheeses

For a change of pace, some familiar mild cheeses also come in flavored versions. Danish Havarti flavored with dill is deservedly popular. Various countries make a caraway-studded cheese called Kuminost. Monterey Jack comes in loaves of quite a few flavors, including jalapeño pepper, good for instant quesadillas. Various herb and garlic-flavored cheese spreads, of which French Boursin is the archetype, make good, simple sandwich spreads.

Blue Cheeses

See page 23.

Mozzarella and Provolone

Both these cheeses are made by cooking, kneading, and pulling the cheese curds so that they form strings, giving the cheese a definite grain. Provolone is then aged. At its best, mozzarella is a delicately sweet, tender cheese that melts well and marries beautifully with the taste of ripe tomatoes. At its worst (the usual supermarket form) it is rather tasteless and rubbery. When buying fresh mozzarella, look for the genuine Italian article, especially the *bufala* type made from buffalo milk. Do also check at a well-stocked cheese shop to see if someone is making good fresh mozzarella in your area. It may be expensive, but it's worth it. Polly-O, from Long Island, is the only supermarket brand I can recommend.

The firmer texture of provolone makes it a favorite cheese for slicing; it's a sandwich-counter staple. I don't much care for it, however.

Dutch Cheeses

Edam and Gouda are two closely related and world-famous cheeses; they are fine partners to sliced meats in a sandwich. Both are smooth-textured, slightly nutty, and noticeably but not overly salty. The loaf- or ball-shaped Edam is a little softer and milder in flavor than the wheel-shaped Gouda. Only the younger Goudas (typically coated with red wax) are easily sliced for sandwiches; aged versions in yellow wax are harder table cheeses.

Storing Cheese

Although cheese is stable at room temperature, it will keep better in the refrigerator. The warmer parts of a refrigerator, the

upper shelves and doors, are good spots for it. To avoid mold or drying, discard the original wrapping and rewrap cheese tightly with plastic wrap after each use (see page 15). A little mold on the surface of firm cheeses can be cut away with a knife or cheese slicer; clean the knife carefully after each cut to avoid smearing the mold all over the freshly cut surface. Even with the best wrapping and clean handling, cheese is best used within a week after you buy it; try to buy no more than you can use in a week.

SPREADS AND CONDIMENTS

A sandwich spread has two purposes, to moisten the bread (and sometimes the filling) and to compliment the flavors of the other ingredients. The most important spreads are mayonnaise and mustard. (Some would add catsup to the list, but there's not much to say about catsup.) Also included here is a discussion of olive oil, which is an important condiment and ingredient in many of the recipes in this book.

Mayonnaise

One of the great master sauces of French cuisine, mayonnaise is a thick emulsion of egg yolks and oil seasoned with vinegar or lemon juice. It has become indispensible to many sandwich cooks. Commercial mayonnaise is generally a very good product, but I sometimes make my own when I want to vary the flavor (see recipe, page 95). The choice of oil in particular defines the flavor. The presence of olive oil is especially identifiable; whether that is desirable or not is a matter of taste.

For those concerned about fat and cholesterol, there is an ever-increasing diversity of reduced-fat, reduced-calorie mayonnaise products available, including some with no cholesterol at all. If one of them is to your liking, fine. For myself, I stick to the original and use it in moderation.

Mustard

Mustard vies with mayonnaise in sandwich popularity, and it wins hands-down in terms of available variety. The various forms of mustard seed (white, brown, and black) combine with an assortment of liquids (water, vinegar, and wine, to name a few) and additional seasonings to create a huge array of mustards, most of which are packaged by someone or other. Like most Americans, I grew up on ballpark or "salad" mustard, made bright yellow by turmeric. I learned to like stronger, browner, and grainier varieties as an adult.

With so many producers putting out bottled mustards, you could probably buy a new variety once a week for the rest of your life without repeating. But a few types stand out.

In fine-grained mustards the seeds are ground to a powder and the prepared mustard has a smooth consistency. Dijon mustard (named after the French city of its origin) sets the standard. It is made from brown mustard and white wine (although *Larousse Gastronomique* says the liquid is verjuice, the acidic, unfermented juice of unripe grapes); it is rather strong in flavor.

Coarse-grained mustards contain cracked or whole mustard seeds. The best known French examples come from Meaux and Bordeaux. These are usually recommended to accompany sausages and pâtés rather than for spreading on sandwiches; for one thing, you need to use rather a lot to cover a piece of bread evenly. If you like a lot of mustard on a sandwich and enjoy hitting little nuggets of mustard flavor (as I do), by all means use them.

There are also innumerable flavored mustards on the market, containing everything from tarragon (a good idea) to pink peppercorns (a bad idea). Experiment with any that appeal to you, but keep in mind that you are adding another flavor to your sandwich and make sure it is compatible with the rest of the ingredients.

Although mustard can be stored at room temperature, it will keep its color and flavor better if refrigerated.

Olive Products

Olives as ingredients or garnish are discussed under Finishing Touches (see page 14). A spread of chopped or mashed olives can be a sandwich filling in itself, or a condiment for another sandwich filling. The most famous example is the Provençal *tapenade,* which is sold in small jars in some specialty food stores. To make your own, see page 94.

If the fruit of the olive is important, its juice—olive oil—is essential. Fine olive oils are available from Spain, France, Italy, Greece, other Mediterranean countries, and California. Within each country there may be dozens of brands from various regions. All this dizzying variety can be reduced to two basic types: virgin oil and everyday oil.

Virgin olive oil is made from the first cold pressing of top-quality ripe olives and is very low in the acids that can give a harsh flavor to olive oil. Most oil-producing countries have legal standards for the maximum acid content which will qualify for the labels "virgin" or "extra virgin." The color, aroma, and flavor of these oils vary by region as well as by brand, from the delicate, almost sweet yellow oils of Nice and Provence to the deep green, peppery oils of Tuscany. Spanish, Greek, and other Italian virgin oils generally fall between these extremes, and are often the best buys as well.

What I call everyday oil is made from higher-acid oils, such as those from later pressings or lower-grade olives, which are then refined to smooth out the rough edges. The refining process also takes away much of the distinctive olive flavor and aroma, leaving a rather neutral oil, so most producers blend a small amount of virgin oil back in to add character. The result is "pure olive oil," the familiar version sold in supermarkets everywhere. Try various brands until you find a favorite. (I mostly use the Sasso brand from Italy.)

For marinades and dressings where you want a strong flavor of the olive, use virgin oil; for cooking, use the everyday variety. Heating a fine virgin oil to cooking temperatures will make your kitchen smell wonderful, but it won't do much for the food, because the volatile aromas of the olive evaporate quickly.

Store all olive oils in tightly sealed containers, away from light and heat. Large cans are much less expensive than smaller sizes. Keep what you need for everyday use in a small oil pitcher near the stove, and reseal the can (with plastic wrap if necessary) to replenish it. Decanting the oil from the can into perfectly clean, dry wine bottles with good corks is an especially good way to keep it.

Bottled Condiments

Mexican-style salsas, relishes, chutneys, and similar condiments can also give a lift to a sandwich. Because most of them are rather high in acid, don't use them in combination with any other sour or strong-flavored condiments.

FINISHING TOUCHES

Good bread, a tasty filling, and a complementary spread make an *almost* complete sandwich. All it takes to bring it to glorious completion is a bit of greenery or tomato for flavor or texture, and something colorful and tasty to garnish the plate.

Lettuce and Other Greens

A leaf of lettuce can add texture, flavor, and color to a sandwich, as well as keeping moist filling ingredients from soaking through the bread. Some of the recipes in this book specify a particular type of lettuce; otherwise, use your choice of crisp head lettuces or leafy types such as butter, red leaf, or oak leaf. For shredding, you need a crisp type. Iceberg gives the mildest flavor; romaine is a little stronger.

Other greens can add a stronger flavor to a sandwich than lettuce. Try arugula, a peppery-bitter green also known as rocket or roquette, to give a boost to a sandwich of mild ingredients or to offset other strong flavors (see Dried Tomato, Cream Cheese, and Arugula Sandwich, page 23). Watercress, curly endive (chicory, frisée), and escarole are also useful when the sandwich calls out for a touch of bitterness rather than the mild sweetness of lettuce.

Tomatoes

Since tomatoes are such a popular sandwich element, one basic fact bears repeating: Tomatoes that are picked green for long shipping and shelf life will never have the flavor of vine-ripened, locally grown tomatoes. From when they first appear in mid-summer to the first frost, local tomatoes are the only ones you should consider. The rest of the year, approach any tomatoes with suspicion, and be prepared for even the best-looking of them to be disappointing.

If you have had trouble with whole tomato slices slipping out of sandwiches with the first bite, here's a trick to remember: Before slicing, score the sides of the tomato with four or five very shallow vertical cuts, just deep enough to cut the skin. With these breaks in the skin of each slice, you should be able to take a bite of the sandwich without the rest of the tomato slice landing on your chin.

Pickles

A crunchy pickle spear is an automatic accompaniment to many deli sandwiches; it provides great flavor and texture contrast.

(I used to put sliced pickles into hamburgers and other sand-wiches when I was a teenager, but in the wisdom of maturity I have learned to appreciate the flavors separately.) Whether you prefer dill or sweet, crunchy or soft pickles is up to you, but for my money the best pickles are the large, crisp, never-cooked type, either kosher dills or half-sour. Tiny gherkins or *cornichons* are also nice as a garnish. I prefer the imported French and German versions which are a quarter-inch in diam-eter; the larger domestic gherkins just seem like undersized pickles.

Olives

Olives show up as ingredients in quite a few of the recipes in this book; they are also a favorite garnish for sandwiches. The color, flavor, and texture of olives are determined by three fac-tors: the variety of olive, when it is picked (green and under-ripe, or purplish-black and fully ripe), and how it is cured (dry, in brine, or in lye). In most cases the recipes specify a color and process rather than a specific olive.

When brine-cured black olives are called for, I recom-mend either the large purplish Kalamata from Greece or the small, thin-meated but fine-flavored Niçoise from France. I am told that the rounder, lighter-colored Royal Victoria from Greece is nearly identical in flavor to the Kalamata. You might also find small Ligurian olives, which come from the part of Italy closest to France and resemble Niçoises. Wrinkled, dry-cured black olives from various sources make an excellent ac-companiment to sandwiches; they are often called Greek-style and sometimes come packed in olive oil.

Among brine-cured green olives, I use both Spanish and California brands, including the ubiquitous pimiento-stuffed variety. Personally, I don't have much use for California "black ripe" olives, which, despite the name, are picked green and processed to make them black. Even the best ones taste a lit-tle soapy to me.

Peppers

Pickled peppers, including cherry peppers and Italian-style *peperoncini*, are also popular as a sandwich garnish. *Peperon-cini* are often tucked inside subs. If you like the little surprise of vinegar followed by hot pepper flavor in your sandwich, by all means include them. Again, I prefer them on the side, to be nibbled more deliberately.

Other Garnishes

Don't forget fresh vegetables as garnishes. A radish rose, a few celery or carrot sticks, slices of jícama, or fresh cucumber spears can supply pleasing color and crunch. If you are watching your salt intake, these plain vegetables are a much better choice than pickles or olives.

TOOLS AND TECHNIQUES

You don't need much in the way of specialized equipment or skills to make great sandwiches. Most of the tools a sandwich maker needs are already found in the average kitchen.

Knives

A good sharp knife is essential, for slicing ingredients and cut-ting up finished sandwiches. The most versatile is a French chef's knife, with a blade 8 to 10 inches long and wide enough that your knuckles don't hit the cutting board when you slice. A paring knife with a 3- to 4-inch blade is handy for peeling and other close work. Many department stores and cutlery shops sell top-quality German and French knives at competitive prices, often in sets which include an intermediate-size "utility knife," sort of a scaled-down chef's knife. This size is useful for cutting cheese; some cooks like it for a whole range of slicing tasks. High-carbon stainless steel blades are best; the non-stainless variety is cheaper and slightly easier to sharpen but can react chemically with tomatoes, onions, and some other ingredients, staining both knives and food.

Learn to use a sharpening steel to keep two or three basic knives sharp, and you can dispense with the cheap or gimmicky tomato slicers and other knives that clutter up most kitchen drawers. A good test of sharpness is whether you can slice a tomato without crushing it.

Unless you use exclusively sliced bread, you will also need a bread knife. This is one case in which a serrated knife works better than a plain blade. Any serrated blade longer than 9 inches will do.

Slicers

Cheese that is difficult to slice evenly with a knife is best cut with a cheese slicer. For firm cheeses such as cheddar, Swiss and Dutch types, and most Danish cheeses, a Scandinavian-style cheese plane does a good job, pulling off well-formed (if somewhat narrow) slices. The plane sticks on some softer cheeses and tears rather than cutting, so for those I go to the type of slicer with a wire and roller. The wire type is not up to cutting the hardest cheddars and Goudas, however.

Spatula

If you make a lot of sandwiches, a short spreading spatula with a rounded edge is handy for applying mayonnaise, mustard, and other spreads. An ordinary table knife or butter knife can do the job, however, as can any small rubber spatula.

Wrapping

If you're going to keep your sandwiches for more than a few minutes before serving, they should be wrapped to prevent the bread from going stale and the filling from drying out. Plastic sandwich bags are fine for normal, squarish sandwiches; but I can't imagine functioning without a good-sized roll of commercial plastic wrap. This stuff comes in 1,000-foot rolls (about a year's supply) and costs a fraction of what the supermarket variety costs—and it works much better. It is ideal not only for wrapping finished sandwiches, but also for storing cheeses, meats, and all other foods.

Storing

Most cold sandwiches can be made ahead of time. You can make tomorrow's lunch tonight so long as you wrap it properly and refrigerate it. An exception is the sandwich with really wet ingredients, such as sliced tomatoes, which will eventually soak through the bread. The best strategy is probably to wrap wet ingredients separately and tuck them into the sandwich just before eating.

A slight disadvantage of making sandwiches the night before is that bread tends to go stale faster in the refrigerator than at room temperature. Maybe slicing and assembling the ingredients the night before will save you enough time that you can make the sandwich in the morning.

Transporting

An insulated cooler is best for picnics, or when you will be transporting sandwiches for several hours in a car or storing them where there is no refrigerator. Just remember to pack them high enough in the cooler that they can't get crushed or soaked in melting ice.

Sandwich Safety

Few lunch boxes, school lockers, or backpacks are refrigerated, so it's important for the sandwich maker to know a bit about food safety and food spoilage. The two most important principles are keeping temperatures cool and avoiding cross-contamination.

To minimize the growth of bacteria and other organisms that can cause food spoilage or food-borne illness, remember the basic formula 4-40-140: Perishable foods should spend no more than 4 hours at a temperature between 40 and 140 degrees Fahrenheit. (Higher temperatures kill spoilage organisms, and lower temperatures keep them from growing.) By the end of four hours, bacteria may have multiplied to unsafe levels. The effect is cumulative, so food that has sat out at room temperature for two hours and then been returned to the refrigerator has only another two hours of room-temperature shelf life left unless it has been cooked again.

What are perishable foods? Basically, those which are high in protein and moisture but low in acid, salt, or sugar (all of which are preservatives). Highly salted or dry-cured meats, such as prosciutto or dry salami, and most cheeses can stand room temperature much better than, say, home-cooked turkey breast or egg salad. Incidentally, mayonnaise has gotten a bad rap in terms of spoilage. Many cooks have an extreme fear of putting mayonnaise into sandwiches that will be out of refrigeration for more than a matter of minutes, fearing that it will spoil quickly. In fact, commercial mayonnaise contains enough vinegar to prevent spoilage for hours. (This is not necessarily true of homemade mayonnaise.) The meat will probably spoil sooner than the mayonnaise. In any case, observe the four-hour rule and you should be safe.

In practical terms, a sandwich made in the morning from properly stored ingredients and taken to school or work should be fine at noon—but it is suspect by midafternoon.

The other principle to remember in sandwich making (as in all cooking) is to avoid cross-contamination, that is, reinfecting cooked foods with bacteria from raw foods (mostly meats). Prevention is simple. Tools, hands, and surfaces used for handling raw meats need to be thoroughly washed before being used for any food that will not be cooked. Most delicatessens do not sell raw meats, but if they do, they should have separate handling areas (including slicers, if appropriate) for raw and cooked items.

COLD SANDWICHES

Leg of Lamb Sandwich with Roasted Garlic
(recipe, page 20)

Muffuletta

No trip to New Orleans is complete without a muffuletta, the Crescent City's greatest contribution to the world of sandwiches. As prepared by the Central Grocery, which made it famous, a muffuletta is an assortment of Italian-style meats and cheeses and a salad of olives and marinated vegetables all piled inside a round, sesame-seed-topped loaf of bread which is then cut into quarters. This version contains a more-or-less traditional combination of meats, but I have substituted a Scandinavian Fontina cheese for the usual Swiss and provolone. The choice of meats and cheeses can be varied endlessly (try lean pastrami or corned beef in place of some of the ham and salami) but it has to have the olive salad to be called a muffuletta.

Serves 4 to 6

- 1 jar (16 ounces) mixed pickled vegetables (*giardiniera*)
- ½ cup pitted green olives
- 1 tablespoon minced garlic
- 3 tablespoons olive oil
- 1 round soft French or Italian bread with sesame seeds, about 1 pound (see Note)
- 4 ounces thinly sliced dry salami
- 4 ounces thinly sliced smoked ham
- 4 ounces sliced Swedish or Danish Fontina

1. Drain the vegetables and olives and cut everything into small dice. Combine with the garlic and olive oil. (The salad may be made up to 2 days ahead and refrigerated.)

2. Slice the bread in half horizontally. Arrange alternating layers of meat and cheese on the bottom half of the loaf, then spread on the olive salad. Cover with the top of the loaf. For the best flavor, wrap the sandwich and let it stand at least 2 hours at room temperature, or refrigerate it for up to 24 hours (remove it from the refrigerator 2 hours before serving). Cut the loaf into quarters or wedges to serve.

NOTE If there is a Greek market in your area, you might find a ring-shaped bread topped with sesame seeds. In the San Francisco Bay Area, some of the Italian bakeries make one and call it Greek bread. If you cannot get a round loaf, make the sandwich on a long French loaf or individual seeded rolls; it may not look authentic, but it will still taste good.

Tuna Muffuletta

In place of the olive-and-*giardiniera* salad of the traditional muffuletta, this sandwich has an olive-studded variation on tartar sauce; instead of meats and cheese, it has thin tuna cutlets. Yet, as different as it is, it still has the spirit of a muffuletta. Yellowfin and bigeye tunas (both of which may be sold under the Hawaiian name *ahi*) are best in flavor and texture. This sandwich will also work with other firm steak fish, such as swordfish or shark.

Serves 4

- ¼ cup mixed pickled vegetables (*giardiniera*), drained
- 6 pitted green olives
- 1 teaspoon minced garlic
- ¼ cup mayonnaise
- 1 pound thick tuna steaks (at least ¾ inch thick)
  Salt and freshly ground pepper
- 1 tablespoon olive oil
  Sliced tomatoes (optional)
- 4 soft French rolls or sections of baguette
  OR 8 slices Pane all'Olio (see page 86)
  or other crusty white bread

1. Chop the vegetables and olives together into very fine dice (⅛- to ¼-inch pieces). Combine them with the garlic and mayonnaise. Set the mixture aside for an hour or so to let the flavors develop.

2. Cut the tuna steaks into ¼-inch-thick slices as described in step 1 of Swordfish Sandwich with Tapenade, page 30. Season the slices with salt and pepper. Heat a heavy skillet over high heat and add the oil. Add the tuna slices a few at a time and saute them until just cooked, 45 seconds to a minute per side. Remove them from the pan and set them aside to cool to room temperature, or wrap and refrigerate them for longer storage.

3. Spread the bread with the mayonnaise mixture and lay a single layer of tuna in each sandwich. Add tomatoes if desired. Serve immediately if the tuna is still warm. If you want to keep the sandwiches to eat later, be sure to make them with thoroughly cooled tuna.

VARIATION For a somewhat different flavor, you can grill the tuna slices on either an outdoor grill or a ridged grilling skillet.

Leg of Lamb Sandwich with Roasted Garlic

Whether you roast lamb in an oven or in an outdoor barbecue, it's an easy matter to put in a couple of whole heads of garlic to roast alongside the meat. When cooked whole, garlic takes on a mild, smooth, nutty taste that can be a revelation to those who know only its stronger side. Even in this milder form, garlic maintains its affinity for lamb, and here it becomes a spread for sandwiches made from the leftovers. A salad of cooked white beans in vinaigrette makes a nice accompaniment.

Serves 4

> 2 firm heads garlic, roasted with a leg of lamb
> (see Step 1)
> 2 tablespoons olive oil
> Salt and freshly ground pepper
> ¾ to 1 pound leftover roast leg of lamb,
> thinly sliced
> 8 slices Pane all'Olio (page 86),
> Walnut Yeasted Bread (page 89),
> OR other crusty bread
> Curly endive or arugula leaves

1. Forty-five minutes before the leg of lamb is done roasting, put the garlic heads in the oven in a small pan or on a square of foil. They are done when light brown juices ooze out from the top. (If cooking the lamb on a covered charcoal grill, place the garlic right on the grill, away from the direct heat, and cook until the skin is nearly blackened and the outer cloves are quite soft.)

2. Set the garlic aside until cool enough to handle, then brush away any burnt skin, and slice each head in half horizontally (across all of the cloves). Squeeze all the cloves out into a bowl and mash them with a fork. Stir in the oil and season to taste with salt and pepper. Cover and refrigerate until the next day; remove from the refrigerator 30 minutes before serving.

3. For each sandwich, spread two slices of bread with the garlic paste; arrange lamb slices and greens on one slice and top with the other. Serve at room temperature.

Party-Size Hero Sandwich

Whether you call it a hero, a submarine, a hoagie, a grinder, or some other regional name, a well-stuffed sandwich on a long roll is an all-American favorite. When you have a gang to feed, instead of making a lot of sandwiches, why not make just a few big ones? Use whole French loaves to make super-size sandwiches, and either cut them into sections or set them out whole with a bread knife so everybody can cut off as much as he or she wants.

Hero sandwiches in delis are often a catchall affair—containing whatever combination of meats they sliced too much of that day. I prefer a more careful assortment of meats that really work together, some milder, some stronger, and a cheese that does not compete. I particularly like the combination given here. Feel free to add, subtract, or substitute meats and cheeses. Save the pickles, peppers, and onions for those who want to add them to their own portions.

Serves 10

> 2 long French loaves, 1 to 1½ pounds each
> 3 to 4 tablespoons mayonnaise
> 3 to 4 tablespoons mustard of your choice
> 6 ounces sliced ham
> 6 ounces thinly sliced dry salami (plain or pepper-coated)
> 6 ounces sliced mortadella
> 6 ounces thinly sliced mild or hot coppa
> 8 ounces sliced Edam, mild Gouda, or Jack cheese
> 1 large or 2 small tomatoes, scored and sliced
> Lettuce leaves, either tender or crisp

Split the loaves lengthwise; spread the bottom halves with mayonnaise, the top halves with mustard. Arrange the meats in even layers on the bread bottoms, in the order given (alternating lighter and darker colors, lighter and denser textures). Fold the meats as necessary so they don't hang sloppily out the sides of the sandwich, and try to make the thickness of each layer as even as possible from end to end. Top the meats with a layer of cheese, then tomatoes and lettuce, then the tops of the loaves. Cut crosswise into sandwiches, or set out whole or half loaves on a long cutting board with a knife.

Blue Cheese and Pears on Walnut Bread

Tangy blue cheese, sweet juicy pears, and crunchy walnuts are a traditional, and delicious, combination. They also make a terrific sandwich. Use whatever blue cheese is your favorite—a classic French Roquefort, Italian Gorgonzola, or not-too-ripe English Stilton, or one of the lesser-known types such as Danish blue, Maytag Blue from Iowa, Oregon blue, French Bleu d'Auvergne, or the luscious Cambozola from Germany, a sort of blue-veined double-cream Brie.

Serves 4

    6 ounces blue cheese
    8 slices Walnut Yeasted Bread (see page 89)
    1 ounce softened cream cheese,
        regular or low-fat (optional)
    2 medium pears, ripe but firm
        Red-leaf or butter lettuce (optional)

1.   If using a soft, spreadable cheese like Gorgonzola, spread it on half the bread slices. If the cheese is of an easily sliced texture, use thin slices. If it is an especially crumbly cheese, break it into chunks and fold it into the cream cheese. Don't mash it too much; it should still be recognizable as blue cheese.

2.   Halve and core the pears; peel them only if the skin is especially gritty (as Comice pears often are). Slice each half into wedges a little less than ¼ inch thick at the bottom and arrange them on top of the cheese. Add lettuce leaves if desired and top with the rest of the bread.

VARIATION   For tea sandwiches, use 12 slices of Quick Nut Bread (see page 90) made with walnuts. Spread the cheese carefully, as the bread is tender; a knife or spreader dipped in hot water and wiped dry can help with spreading crumbly cheese. Slice the pears more thinly (about ⅛ inch thick) and omit the lettuce. Makes 2 dozen squares.

Dried Tomato, Cream Cheese, and Arugula Sandwich

Italian-style sun-dried tomatoes (*pumate*) preserve the summery flavor of fully ripe tomatoes so that it can be enjoyed from fall to spring, when vine-ripened fresh tomatoes are not available. This sandwich combines sun-dried tomatoes with arugula, a peppery-tasting green that is also at its best in spring and fall.

Serves 4

    8 sun-dried tomato halves, oil-packed (see Note)
    6 ounces cream cheese
        Salt and freshly ground pepper
    ½ cup arugula leaves (also called rocket or roquette)
    1 seeded baguette, about ¾ pound, split

Drain and chop the tomatoes. Beat the cream cheese with a wooden spoon until it is soft and easily spreadable. Stir in the chopped tomatoes and season to taste with salt and pepper (no salt may be needed with some brands of dried tomatoes). Spread the mixture on the bottom half of the bread, add a generous layer of arugula, and top it with the top of the loaf. Cut the sandwich into quarters to serve.

NOTE   Italian sun-dried tomatoes packed in olive oil are expensive, but they go a long way, and they really are better than any alternative I know of. If you want to save money, you can buy the dried tomatoes loose, soak and drain them, and pack them in oil yourself. Place the dried tomatoes in a bowl, add just enough boiling water to cover, and let them stand until they swell and thoroughly soften, about 45 minutes. Or, to save time, you can simmer them in a small saucepan until soft. Let the tomatoes cool, then drain and chop them. Use them immediately or pack them in olive oil. Be sure the oil completely covers the tomatoes, and plan to use them rather quickly.

NOTE   If you cannot get a seeded baguette, a plain baguette is the next best choice. Four poppy-seed bagels are another option, but their texture really isn't the same. And don't be tempted to serve bagels this way for breakfast—they're too strong in flavor to eat first thing in the morning.

Blue Cheese and Pears on Walnut Bread

Maine Lobster Roll

In Maine, where lobster is plentiful and cheap enough to be fast food, lobster sandwiches are a popular item at walk-away food stands. Cold lobster salad is tucked into a hot dog roll which has been browned on a griddle until crisp outside (the contrast between cold salad and hot roll is crucial). In the rest of the country this tasty sandwich is something of a splurge. Keep an eye out for specials on live lobster; culls, lobsters missing one claw, are often available at a bargain price. I have also made this sandwich with spiny lobster from southern California, and it was delicious.

Serves 4

       1 cooked lobster (about 1½ pounds), or ½ pound
          cooked lobster meat
      ½ cup finely chopped celery
       3 tablespoons mayonnaise
      ½ teaspoon Dijon or other strong mustard
          (optional; it's not traditional, but I like it)
       2 teaspoons oil or butter
       4 hot dog rolls (see Note)

1. Remove the meat from the lobster's tail and claws and cut it into bite-size pieces. Combine it with the celery, mayonnaise, and mustard and chill thoroughly.

2. Heat a skillet or griddle and coat it with oil or melted butter. Brown the white sides of the rolls until golden and crisp. Slice the rolls open (if not already sliced) and spoon the lobster salad inside. Serve immediately.

NOTE To be really authentic, the hot dog rolls should be the kind that come stuck together side by side, so that when you pull or cut them apart you have a squarish roll with a broad band of unbrowned white bread on each side. This is the surface that goes down against the griddle to be browned. If all you can get is the sliced-on-the-side type, trim the sides slightly and grill them.

TECHNIQUE NOTE Opinions vary on the best and most humane way to cook a live lobster. Immersing the lobster head first in boiling water is the most common method. Here is another which some experts feel is more humane, and which produces an especially tender texture. Place the lobster (Maine or spiny) in a deep pot and cover it with cold water. Cover the pot and place it over medium-high heat. When the water comes to a boil, turn off the heat and let the lobster steep 10 minutes. Remove the lobster and chill it, ideally by covering it with ice.

VARIATION To prepare with frozen lobster tail, use one 12-ounce or two 6-ounce tails. Thaw and steam until the meat is opaque, about 8 minutes for small tails and 10 to 12 minutes for larger sizes. Crack or split the shell, remove the meat, discard the central vein, and proceed with step 1 above.

Turkey Waldorf Sandwich

The traditional Waldorf salad—a combination of apples, celery, walnuts, and mayonnaise—has been popular in the United States since the 1890s. Break the salad down into its parts, reassemble them on bread with sliced turkey, and the Waldorf sandwich is born.

Serves 4

       2 heaping tablespoons walnut halves or pieces
      ¼ cup mayonnaise
       1 tart apple
       2 large ribs celery
       8 slices Basic White Bread (page 84),
          Basic Whole Wheat Bread (page 85),
          OR your choice of sliced bread
      12 ounces sliced turkey breast
          Red lettuce leaves (optional)

1. Chop the nuts finely by hand or in a food processor or, better still, grate them with a rotary (Mouli) grater. Stir the chopped nuts into the mayonnaise.

2. Halve and core the apple (do not peel it) and slice it thinly. Slice the celery with long diagonal cuts into the thinnest possible slices.

3. To assemble each sandwich, spread a slice of bread with walnut mayonnaise and add a layer of celery, a layer of turkey, and a layer of apple. Finish with lettuce, if desired, and a second slice of bread.

Grilled Eggplant Sandwich with Fresh Mozzarella

Since I discovered the flavor that grilling brings to eggplant, I have hardly cooked it any other way. In fact, whenever I have the grill fired up I search the refrigerator for vegetables that can be roasted, often with future meals in mind. Leftover grilled slices of eggplant make a delicious sandwich for the next day's lunch.

Serves 4

- 1 clove garlic
- 3 tablespoons fruity olive oil
- 2 small eggplants (about 1½ pounds; see Note)
  Salt and freshly ground pepper
- 8 ounces fresh mozzarella
- 8 slices crusty white bread
  OR a 1-pound baguette, split
- 1 cup (loosely packed) fresh basil leaves

1. Prepare a moderate to hot charcoal fire and preheat the grill thoroughly. Mince or crush the garlic, add it to the olive oil, and let it stand at least 30 minutes while the fire is getting started.

2. Remove the stem ends from the eggplants and cut them crosswise into ¼-inch slices; do not peel them. Grill the slices until well browned on both sides, seasoning them with salt and pepper and brushing them lightly with the garlic-flavored oil as they cook. Allow them to cool in a single layer on a tray or platter; brush them again with oil as they cool. When cool, cover and refrigerate.

3. Slice the cheese thinly across the grain. Season to taste with salt and pepper. For each sandwich, arrange a double layer of eggplant slices on a slice of bread and top with cheese, a generous layer of basil, and another slice of bread. If using a baguette, make one large sandwich and slice it into quarters.

NOTE Look for eggplant with smooth, taut, unblemished skin. The traditional method of salting the raw eggplant to remove bitterness is unnecessary with smaller, less mature specimens. Use the seeds as a guide; if they are small, pale, and undeveloped, the flavor will be milder. If there are many brown, fully formed seeds, salt the slices lightly on both sides and drain them on paper or cloth towels for 15 minutes before cooking.

VARIATION Use 2 or 3 long, slender Japanese or Chinese eggplants, sliced lengthwise.

VARIATION You can serve this sandwich hot, straight from the grill. It is a nice alternative to offer vegetarians at a barbecue.

Prosciutto and Artichoke Hearts on Focaccia

Compared to their American counterparts, European sandwiches tend to go lighter on the meat and heavier on the bread, but what bread! And what meats! I first saw focaccia—the soft, fragrant Italian sheet bread—used as a sandwich bread in a café in the heart of Florence. Inside the split focaccia were a few thin slices of prosciutto. This version also has marinated artichokes. No condiments are really needed, since the artichokes and ham have plenty of flavor and the bread has enough oil. You could add a touch of mustard if you like.

Serves 4

- ½ sheet (1 pound) plain or herb focaccia, bought or homemade (see page 88)
- 2 jars (6 ounces each) marinated artichoke hearts
- 10 to 12 ounces thinly sliced prosciutto or other dry-cured ham

1. (Optional) Warm the focaccia on a baking sheet in a 300° oven until slightly crisp. If the focaccia is very oily, transfer it to a clean sheet lined with paper towels to absorb some of the excess.

2. Drain the artichokes (reserve the marinade for another purpose—it makes a pretty good instant salad dressing). If the artichokes are especially large, split them in half lengthwise. Cut the focaccia into quarters and split each quarter horizontally. Lay the prosciutto on the focaccia bottoms. Arrange the artichokes on top and cover with the focaccia tops. Cut the sandwiches in half diagonally.

Braised Leek Sandwich with Anchovies

Leeks in vinaigrette are a popular cold hors d'oeuvre; why not tuck them inside a French roll for a sandwich? And don't skimp on the anchovies—they are needed to provide a salty accent to the sweetness of the leeks. Like a muffuletta, this sandwich improves with an hour or two of age.

Serves 4

1½ pounds slender leeks
    Water
  1 tablespoon everyday olive oil
  1 teaspoon Dijon-style mustard
  1 teaspoon wine vinegar
    Pinch of salt
    Freshly ground black pepper
  2 tablespoons olive oil (everyday, extra virgin, or a blend)
  4 not-too-crisp French rolls
   OR 4 sections of a 1½-pound French loaf, split
  6 canned anchovy filets, drained

1. Rinse the leeks, trim off the root ends, and remove any dark outer leaves. Trim the tops to where the color begins to change from pale green to deeper green. Slit each leek lengthwise almost to the bottom; roll it a quarter turn and slit it again. Wash the leeks well in a bowl of water, swishing them up and down in the water to dislodge any dirt. Drain the leeks and place them in a heavy covered pot. Cover them with water (you can use some of the washing water once the dirt settles to the bottom); add a tablespoon of oil. Bring the water to a boil, reduce it to a simmer, cover the pot, and cook until the leeks are quite tender, about 15 minutes. Drain the leeks in a colander, then spread them out on a towel to dry further.

2. In a large, shallow bowl, combine the mustard, vinegar, salt, and pepper from a few twists of the pepper mill. Stir with a fork to dissolve the salt, then add the 2 tablespoons of oil and stir well to form a thick dressing. Add the leeks and turn them to coat them with the dressing. (The leeks may be prepared to this point up to a day ahead of time and refrigerated;

remove them from the refrigerator an hour before serving.)

3. Lift the leeks out of the dressing, letting the excess dressing drain back into the bowl. Cut the leeks to convenient lengths and arrange the pieces on the bottom half of the bread or rolls. Coarsely chop the anchovies. Combine them with the dressing remaining in the bowl, and spread this mixture evenly on the top half of the bread. Close the sandwiches and serve immediately, or wrap them for serving later.

Smoked Chicken Sandwich with Pepper Slaw

Moist, tender, and infused with the flavor of hardwood smoke, smoked chicken offers a nice change from barbecued chicken and from other smoked meats. In a sandwich it goes especially well with a crunchy homemade coleslaw of cabbage and sweet pepper. Smoked chickens are available in well-stocked poultry shops and gourmet food stores as well as by mail order. Half a bird will provide plenty of meat for four sandwiches.

Serves 4

  1 cup thinly sliced cabbage
  ½ cup seeded and thinly sliced red pepper (about ½ of a large pepper)
  1 heaping tablespoon mayonnaise
  1 teaspoon mustard
    Salt and pepper (optional)
  8 slices seeded rye bread
    Meat from ½ of a smoked chicken, cut or pulled into coarse shreds (about 1½ cups)

1. Combine the cabbage, red pepper, mayonnaise, and mustard in a bowl and let the mixture stand for approximately 30 minutes. Taste for seasoning and add salt and pepper to taste, if necessary (I like it as is).

2. Spread the cabbage mixture on half of the bread slices. Add a thick layer of shredded chicken to each, and top with a second slice of bread.

Swordfish Sandwich with Tapenade

I love swordfish, but it's expensive, so I am always looking for ways to get it to go farther. Here a Japanese cutting technique turns a thick swordfish steak into two or three thin, quick-cooking cutlets suitable for a sandwich.

There are those who feel that swordfish should be served as plainly as possible, but I like to combine it with full-flavored Mediterranean ingredients like olives, garlic, and anchovies, all of which are combined in the pungent Provençal black-olive spread called tapenade.

Serves 4

> 1 **pound swordfish, in one piece or two thick steaks**
> **Salt and pepper**
> 1 **tablespoon olive oil**
> 2 **teaspoons lemon juice**
> 8 **slices crusty bread, preferably from a round loaf**
> **Tender lettuce leaves**
> ½ **cup Tapenade (see page 94)**

1. Have the swordfish steaks cut into ¼-inch-thick slices at the market, or do it yourself as follows: Lay a pair of Chinese-style bamboo chopsticks on a cutting board just far enough apart to set the steak in between. (Chinese-style chopsticks are the ones with square handles and little or no taper, sold in bundles in Chinese stores.) Press down lightly on the steak with the palm of one hand to hold it in place. Lay your slimmest, sharpest knife horizontally across the chopsticks and slide it the length of the chopsticks, slicing the steak horizontally. Cut as smoothly as possible, ideally with one or two long, drawing cuts, to get a smooth surface. Remove the thin slice and cut again until the whole steak is sliced. (The last slice seldom comes out exactly the same thickness as the others, so remember to give it a few seconds more or less cooking time.)

2. Season the swordfish slices with salt and pepper and cook them (on a grill or a ridged grilling skillet, or in a lightly oiled saute pan) until just done, about a minute per side. To check for doneness, bend a slice until it begins to spread apart and look into the center of the meat; it should show just a trace of pink translucence. Transfer the cooked slices to a platter or baking pan large enough to hold them in a single layer, sprinkle them with olive oil and lemon juice, and turn them to get an even coating. Let the fish cool, or cover and refrigerate it for longer storage.

3. Place lettuce leaves and then swordfish slices on four of the slices of bread. Spread the remaining bread slices generously with tapenade and lay them over the swordfish.

VARIATION Try the same cutting and cooking methods with other firm, meaty fish like sturgeon, shark, or halibut; or use butterflied and pounded chicken breasts (see Grilled Chicken Breast Sandwich with Chile-Orange Mayonnaise, page 41). For turkey breast cutlets, cut crosswise slices ¼ inch thick and pound them to a little more than ⅛ inch.

Nut Butter Sandwiches

There's nothing wrong with peanut butter and jelly sandwiches; I eat them all the time. But when I want a change, I look for other nut butters or make my own (see page 94). And not just any jelly will do; I find that each nut has affinities for particular fruits. Almonds are closely related to peaches and apricots, and almond butter goes beautifully with jams from these fruits. Put apricot jam on cashew butter, on the other hand, and each seems to cancel out the flavor of the other. For the most adult nut butter sandwich of all, try dark brown hazelnut butter with orange marmalade.

Serves 1

> 2 **slices whole wheat bread**
> 1 **to 1½ tablespoons nut butter**
> 1 **tablespoon jam, jelly, or preserves**

Spread one slice of bread with nut butter, add the jam, and top with the other slice of bread.

SUGGESTED COMBINATIONS
- Almond butter and apricot or peach jam
- Cashew butter and blackberry preserves
- Cashew butter and currant jelly
- Hazelnut butter and orange marmalade

Tea Sandwiches

The time-honored tradition of afternoon tea is enjoying a come-back in many urban hotels, and well it should. You don't have to be a white-gloved lady to appreciate a cup of hot tea and a tempting assortment of sandwiches in the middle of the after-noon. Whether you're tired from shopping, working, or chasing the kids, a midafternoon rest and a cup of tea is welcome and energizing. Afternoon tea at home is an easy and relaxing way to entertain friends and neighbors, especially at holiday time when everyone is grateful for an excuse to stop and take a breather. Tea sandwiches are also excellent additions to any party buffet.

To make tea sandwiches in quantity, use whole unsliced loaves of bread and slice them horizontally as described in the recipe for Turkey and Cranberry Roulade on page 66. Figure each horizontal slice from a standard loaf as 2 to 2½ times the size of a regular crosswise slice, and apply the fillings pro-portionately.

If you have to make tea sandwiches a few hours ahead of time, lay them out on serving trays and wrap tray and all in plastic wrap to keep the sandwiches from drying out. Refrigerate only if necessary, as bread goes stale faster in the refrigerator.

Cream Cheese and Chutney Tea Sandwiches

This is a grown-up's version of a cream cheese and jelly sandwich; it gives a little punch to a tray of otherwise mild tea sandwiches. Use any good bottled chutney, either Major Grey's or any other with a similar consistency. (Major Grey's is not a brand name, but a mango-based type of chutney.)

Makes 1 dozen

> 6 slices fine-textured whole wheat bread
>   or good white bread
> 3 tablespoons cream cheese (regular or low-fat),
>   softened
> 3 tablespoons bottled chutney

Spread half the bread slices with cream cheese, then chutney. Cover with the remaining bread and trim off the crusts. Cut each sandwich into quarters.

Cherry Tea Sandwiches

This sandwich was inspired by the traditional cherry sand-wiches of Shaker cookery, which combine pitted cherries, ground almonds, and lots of sugar as a sandwich filling between slices of buttered bread. This variation has the nuts, in this case pecans, right in the bread and replaces the butter with cream cheese. Use sweet cherries such as Bings when they are in season. The rest of the year, use frozen cherries; be sure to drain them well after thawing.

Makes 1 dozen

> 12 slices Quick Nut Bread (page 90) made with pecans
> 4 ounces cream cheese (regular or low-fat),
>   softened
> 1 cup sweet cherries (fresh or thawed),
>   pitted and chopped

Spread all the bread with cream cheese and spread the cher-ries on half the slices. Cover with the remaining slices and trim off the crusts. Cut each sandwich in half.

Sweet Onion Tea Sandwiches

I can only recommend these with the sweetest, mildest onions, the type that just about anyone can eat raw: Vidalias from Georgia, Walla Wallas from Washington, Mauis from Hawaii, and certain supersweet Granex onions from Texas. Each variety is in season for a short time, but the seasons are staggered, so you should be able to find one or another type much of the year.

Makes 1 dozen

    6 slices Egg Bread (page 87) or brioche bread
       (available at some bakeries)
    3 tablespoons unsalted butter, softened
       Pinch of ground cloves
    1 medium sweet onion, peeled

Spread all the bread slices with butter and sprinkle them very lightly with cloves. Cut enough thin slices of onion to cover three of the slices of bread. Top each slice of bread and onion with one of the remaining bread slices and trim off the crusts. Cut each sandwich into quarters.

Cucumber Tea Sandwiches

This is one of the most basic tea sandwiches. Crisp slices of cucumber contrast with the smooth texture of cream cheese, which here replaces the traditional sweet butter. A bit of lemon zest, stirred into the cheese, adds a lively note.

Makes 1 dozen

    ½ small cucumber, peeled and thinly sliced
       Kosher salt
    1 teaspoon grated lemon zest
    4 ounces cream cheese (regular or low-fat), softened
    6 slices good white bread

1. Place the cucumber slices in a shallow bowl and sprinkle them lightly with salt. Let them stand 15 minutes, then rinse them quickly and lay them out to dry between paper towels.

2. Stir the lemon zest into the cream cheese and spread it evenly on all six slices of bread. Top three of the bread slices with overlapping slices of cucumber, then cover each with one of the remaining slices of bread, cheese side down. Trim off the crusts and cut the sandwiches into square or triangular quarters.

Watercress Tea Sandwiches

This sandwich uses ricotta cheese pureed with a little yogurt (the *fromage blanc* of French "diet cuisine") as a less caloric substitute for butter or cream cheese. You won't miss the calories a bit. If there is a Chinatown or a Chinese market near you, that's where you should shop for watercress. It's a favorite Chinese soup ingredient, and Chinese markets always have the freshest and cheapest watercress around.

Makes 1 dozen

    1 cup ricotta cheese
    1 tablespoon plain yogurt
    1 bunch watercress
    6 slices good white bread

1. Combine the ricotta and yogurt in a food processor or blender and process until quite smooth and not a bit grainy, at least a full minute. Stop the machine to scrape down the sides of the container a few times. (The *fromage blanc* may be prepared several days ahead and stored, tightly covered, in the refrigerator.)

2. Remove the thick stems and any battered leaves from the watercress and wash the tops in a bowl of water. Lift them out of the water and drain them thoroughly (a salad spinner works best). Measure a loosely packed cup and reserve the rest for your next tossed green salad. Chop the cup of watercress and stir it into the *fromage blanc*. Spread the mixture thickly on half the bread slices, cover them with the remaining slices, and trim off the crusts. Cut each sandwich into square or triangular quarters.

HOT SANDWICHES

*Zucchini Latkes on Dill Bread
(recipe, page 46)*

The Perfect Hamburger

I don't eat hamburgers anywhere near as often as I used to. But every few weeks, when I get in the mood for a burger, nothing else will do. And it had better be a good one. As you can see from the recipe title, I have pretty strong feelings about what makes a great hamburger. So what follows is as much my personal list of burger do's and don't's as it is a recipe.

Don't assume that the leanest ground beef makes the best burgers. Meat with less than about 20 percent fat will make too dry a hamburger unless you cook it quite rare. The best choice in most supermarkets is the middle grade of ground beef, lean or "ground round" rather than the fattier ground chuck or extra lean "ground sirloin." (I always get a kick out of these labels. Does anybody believe that they are actually grinding up sirloin back there? In fact, most ground beef comes from the chuck, neck, and miscellaneous trimmings. For the regular blend they throw in more fat; for the leaner blends they use less.) Hamburgers cooked on a grill dry out a little faster than those cooked in a skillet or on a griddle, so you need slightly more fat in grilled burgers.

Form hamburgers with as little handling as possible. If you pack the meat too tightly, you will make a hockey puck rather than a hamburger. And whatever you do, don't press down on the meat with a spatula as it cooks; that technique guarantees a dry hamburger. A quarter pound of meat per burger is enough for me these days; allow a third of a pound for bigger appetites.

To season or not to season? Some cooks like to mix salt, pepper, garlic powder, or other seasonings into the meat before cooking. Some even add chopped onions or Worcestershire sauce. Now, I like meat loaf, but I don't expect it when I sit down to a burger. Most of us use some sort of condiments on our hamburgers anyway, so I prefer to keep the patty pristine until it hits the bun. If you want to add salt, add it to the cooked side after turning. (All of the above notwithstanding, one of my favorite variations on a hamburger is a sort of inside-out cheeseburger; see the variation below.)

What to put on the finished hamburger? When I get a hamburger in a restaurant and it comes with lettuce, tomato, and pickle, I eat those things separately, with a knife and fork, as a bit of salad. I sometimes like grilled (never raw) onions on a burger; otherwise, all that goes inside my bun is mustard. Catsup is okay, if you like it.

Serves 4

    1 to 1⅓ pounds lean ground beef
    1 tablespoon oil
    ½ cup sliced onions
    4 onion rolls or Kaiser rolls, split
      Mustard of your choice

1.   Divide the meat into quarters by eye and gently form each quarter into a patty, handling the meat just enough to shape it and round off any corners. Make the patties of an even thickness, about 1 inch thick if you like the meat rare or medium rare, ¾ inch for medium, thinner for (gasp!) well done.

2.   Heat a heavy skillet over medium-low heat and add the oil. Add the onions and cook them, turning the slices occasionally and breaking apart the rings, until well browned. Meanwhile, heat the broiler.

3.   If you have a ridged cast-iron skillet, you can use it as a broiling pan and end up with nice grill marks on one side of your burgers. Heat the pan under the broiler before putting the patties in. If you don't have a ridged skillet, place the patties on the rack of a broiler pan.

4.   Open the rolls and put them on a sheet pan lower in the oven to toast while the meat cooks. Broil the patties 2 to 3 inches from the heat until well browned, about 4 minutes; turn them over, season them if desired, and broil another 3 minutes or so. When red juices begin to run out the edges of the patties the insides will be medium rare. Place the patties on the bottom halves of the buns and add the cooked onions; spread mustard on the top halves of the buns, and close them. Enjoy.

VARIATION For blue-cheese burgers, use up to 1 pound of meat, and carefully form each patty around a 1-ounce slab of firm blue cheese. Make the patties 1 inch thick and cook as above.

Herbed Omelette Sandwich

Several years ago, *Sunset* magazine carried a recipe for a family-size sandwich containing an Italian- or Spanish-style flat omelette. I don't remember what was in their omelette, but the idea has stuck with me. This version uses mushrooms, bacon, and roasted red pepper. You can try it with any ingredients you might put in a frittata: grated or sliced zucchini, cooked asparagus, sliced potatoes, or artichoke hearts, to name a few. This sandwich is equally good hot or at room temperature, making it ideal for a picnic lunch.

Serves 4 to 6

  3 tablespoons olive oil
  ½ pound mushrooms, thickly sliced
  ½ cup sliced green onions, including tops
      Salt and freshly ground black pepper to taste
  1 round, flat loaf French bread (1½ pounds)
  5 large eggs, at room temperature
  1 tablespoon chopped fresh herbs—thyme, chives, chervil, tarragon, parsley, or a blend
  8 slices crisp cooked bacon
  1 large or 2 small red bell peppers or pimientos, roasted, peeled, and cut into wide strips (see Note)

1. Heat 1 tablespoon of the oil over medium heat in a 10-inch skillet (well-seasoned cast iron or nonstick with a heat-proof handle). Add the mushrooms and green onions and cook until they begin to release their liquid, then turn the heat to medium-high and cook until the liquid is nearly gone. Remove the mushrooms from the pan, season them generously with salt and pepper, and set them aside to cool slightly.

2. Split the bread horizontally and pull out most of the inside of each half, leaving a shell no more than ½ inch thick. (Save the pulled-out pieces, let them dry, and crumble them for breadcrumbs.)

3. Beat the eggs lightly in a large bowl. Stir in the mushroom mixture and the herbs. Wipe the skillet clean, add another tablespoon of oil, and return it to medium heat. Pour in the egg mixture, spreading the mushrooms evenly in the pan. Cook until the eggs are set around the edges but still runny in the center, about 5 minutes, then put the pan under the broiler for a minute or two to brown the top and finish cooking the eggs. If the center is still moist after the top browns, return the pan to the stovetop for another minute or so.

4. Slide the omelette out of the pan into the bottom half of the bread. Top with the bacon and roasted pepper, and drizzle with the oil and juices from the pepper. Cover with the top of the loaf. Serve immediately, or wrap in foil to keep warm for up to 3 hours. To serve, cut the sandwich into quarters or wedges.

NOTE To roast and peel peppers, place them whole under a broiler, over a hot charcoal fire, or on a burner directly above a gas flame. Turn the peppers until the skin is evenly blistered all over (most of the skin will blacken, but try not to burn the flesh underneath). Transfer the peppers to a large jar or bowl, cover, and let sit until the peppers wilt. Peel off the burnt skins, slit the peppers open over a bowl (to catch the juices), and remove the seeds and ribs. Cut the peppers into strips, put them in the bowl with the juices, add a tablespoon of olive oil, and season to taste with salt and pepper. Roasted peppers will keep for several days in the refrigerator.

Chinese Roast Duck Sandwich

The Chinese are the best duck roasters in the world. If you live near a Chinatown, chances are there is a Chinese delicatessen selling Cantonese-style roast ducks. Otherwise, check with local restaurants that serve Peking duck; they may be willing to sell you a whole duck to go. Be sure to specify that you want the duck whole, not cut up, or you may find yourself with a cartonful of chopstick-size chunks with bones.

Serves 4 to 6

- ½ cup boiling water
- 1½ ounces (about ⅓ cup) dried apricot halves
- 1 tablespoon minced fresh ginger
- 1½ teaspoons sugar
- 1 teaspoon cider vinegar or rice vinegar
- 1 teaspoon soy sauce
- ½ teaspoon cornstarch
- 1 Chinese roast duck
- 1 bunch watercress
- 4 to 6 large soft rolls or 8 to 12 small dinner rolls, warmed in the oven and sliced open

1. In a small bowl, pour the boiling water over the apricots and let them stand until cool. Drain the water into a small saucepan. Dice the apricots finely and add them to the water along with the ginger, sugar, and vinegar. Simmer until the liquid is reduced by half. Mix the soy sauce with a tablespoon of cool water and dissolve the cornstarch in it. Add the soy sauce mixture to the apricot sauce; cook it until glossy and slightly thickened. Transfer the sauce to a bowl and keep it warm.

2. Carve the duck, first cutting away the breast and leg meat in large pieces with the skin attached. Set these aside while you carve as much of the meaty bits from the carcass as you have the patience for. (Save the carcass and simmer it in chicken stock for a delicious soup.) Arrange the skinless pieces on a serving plate, then slice the breast and leg meat into thin strips, each with a little skin attached, and arrange them attractively on top. Garnish the platter with watercress.

3. To serve, set out the duck, apricot sauce, rolls, and either chopsticks or forks. Let each person tuck some duck inside a sliced roll, add a little sauce, and eat it sandwich-style. The watercress is not just for looks; its peppery flavor is a nice counterpart to the duck. Add a sprig to each sandwich or nibble it separately (my preference).

VARIATION In restaurants, Peking duck is often served with thin Mandarin pancakes, eggless crepes which are available in Chinese markets. You can use them instead of rolls to wrap up the duck and sauce. Flour tortillas also work very well. Warm either on a dry skillet just before serving. Another option is a plain (unfilled) Chinese bun or *bao*, either baked or steamed. If there is a Chinese bakery or teahouse in the neighborhood, they may make some unfilled *bao* for you if you order them in advance.

Grilled Chicken Breast Sandwich with Chile-Orange Mayonnaise

Chicken paillards, butterflied boneless breast halves pounded to the thickness of scaloppine, are amazingly quick to grill. They are on and off the fire in about two minutes, making them especially useful when you have a lot of people to feed. Or, if you're cooking for just a few people, you can get by with a small fire in a single-grill hibachi.

Serves 4

- ¼ cup mayonnaise, bottled or homemade (see page 95)
- 2 teaspoons ancho, California, or New Mexico chile powder (see Note)
- 2 teaspoons grated orange peel
- 1 to 2 tablespoons orange juice
- 2 whole chicken breasts
  Peanut or other vegetable oil
  Salt and freshly ground pepper
- 8 slices Pane all'Olio (page 86) or other crusty white bread
  Shredded lettuce

1. Combine the mayonnaise, chile powder, orange peel, and orange juice to taste. Set aside at least 30 minutes to allow the flavors to blend. Refrigerate for longer storage.

2. Skin, split, and bone the chicken breasts. Find the seam between the two muscles on each breast half with a fingertip. Cut through the membrane that attaches the two muscles on the breastbone side, but leave them attached on the rib side. Fold the smaller muscle back to form a lopsided heart shape.

3. Sprinkle a butterflied breast with a little oil and place it on a sheet of oiled waxed paper or a clean plastic bag. Top with another sheet of oiled paper or plastic. Pound with a meat pounder, a mallet, or the side of a heavy cleaver to a thickness of ⅛ inch. The piece should nearly double in area. Repeat with the other breast halves. Sprinkle the paillards with a little more oil, salt, and pepper and set aside until ready to grill. (The chicken may be prepared to this point an hour to a day ahead of time and refrigerated; remove from the refrigerator 15 minutes before cooking.)

4. Prepare a hot charcoal fire and preheat the grill thoroughly. Toast the bread lightly on the grill if desired. Spread each slice with mayonnaise. Grill the chicken paillards over a hot fire just until opaque, about 1 minute per side. Cut each paillard in half if necessary to fit on a slice of bread. Top the chicken with shredded lettuce and a second bread slice.

NOTE Pure chile powder *(chile molido)* is nothing but whole dried chiles finely ground. It is not to be confused with chili powder, which may also contain garlic, oregano, cumin, and other seasonings. Several varieties of chile powder are sold in Mexican markets and supermarkets wherever there is a Mexican population. California chile is the mildest, New Mexico somewhat hotter; *chile ancho* is the hottest of the common varieties but also the richest in flavor.

VARIATION If you want a stronger chile flavor on the chicken itself, or you want to cut back or eliminate the mayonnaise, dust the chicken with chile powder after pounding. It will stain the oil (and the chicken) an attractive orange color.

Torta Mexicana

The Mexican-style sandwich known as a *torta* is not as well known as tacos and burritos (see page 74), although it is sold at many of the same *taquerías*. Scooping the middle out of an oval roll *(bolillo)* makes a pocket ready for a savory stuffing of beans, meat, cheese, and salsa. Be sure to get a roll with some character, not an oval of balloon bread. If there is a Mexican bakery near you, it should have some sort of *bolillos*.

Serves 4

  4 oval sandwich rolls
  1 cup cooked pinto or black turtle beans,
    mashed or refried, warm (see Note)
  ½ cup grated Jack or Muenster cheese (optional)
  1 cup Carnitas, Chilorio, or one of the other fillings
    on pages 77-78
  1 cup shredded romaine or iceberg lettuce
    Fresh Tomato Salsa (page 96) or bottled
    tomato salsa, to taste

1. Split the rolls along one side, if not already split, and open them. Pull out some of the bread from both the top and bottom halves, leaving a cavity almost the full length of the roll. (Instead of discarding the pulled-out pieces, let them dry and crumble them for breadcrumbs.)

2. Spread a layer of beans in the bottom of each roll, then add a layer of cheese and one of filling. Fill the tops of the rolls with lettuce and salsa and close the sandwiches. Cut in half if desired.

NOTE To get the texture of refried beans with a fraction of the fat, simply place cooked beans in a skillet with some of their cooking liquid and mash with a potato masher while cooking over low heat. Let the mixture thicken to the desired texture. You can also make this sandwich with well-drained unmashed beans, especially if you are using a smaller variety like black turtle beans.

Torta Mexicana filled with
Chilorio (page 78)

East Carolina Barbecue Sandwich

Politically the Carolinas may be divided north and south, but to barbecue aficionados the key division is east and west. That the meat is pork is a given; it's the sauce that tells you where you are. In the Blue Ridge mountains in the west, the sauce is thick with tomatoes, but where the foothills level out into the Piedmont and the coastal plain, it's a clear red liquid, mostly vinegar and red pepper. The meat is cooked slowly over hardwood, as plainly as can be—without even salt and pepper. Then it is chopped into bits and seasoned with the fiery sauce. Piled into a bun, it makes a hearty sandwich.

Coleslaw is a traditional accompaniment to Carolina barbecue. Some say it should go inside the sandwich, while others blanch at the thought of anything but the sauce touching their barbecue. Try it both ways and decide for yourself.

Note that you'll need two charcoal grills to cook the meat, one covered, the other a small open grill.

Serves 8

1½ **cups hardwood smoking chips such as hickory or oak**
 1 **pork shoulder or Boston butt roast, 2 to 3 pounds**
 ½ **cup cider vinegar**
1½ **tablespoons crushed red pepper**
    Salt
 8 **hamburger buns or other soft rolls**
 4 **cups coleslaw**

1. *Eight to nine hours ahead of serving,* build a small charcoal fire (about 25 briquets) on one side of a covered kettle-type barbecue grill. Let the charcoal burn until covered with a light layer of ash. Transfer 2 or 3 of the glowing briquets to another small grill or hibachi and add 5 more briquets to this second grill.

2. Place a disposable drip pan with 1 inch of water in the kettle grill, beneath the grilling rack on the side opposite the fire. Position the rack so that you will be able to add charcoal to the fire later (there is usually an opening near each handle). Cover the grill and open or close the vents as necessary to bring the temperature to 225° to 250°. (An instant-reading thermometer suspended through one of the top vent holes gives a constant reading of the temperature without your having to open the grill.)

3. When the temperature is right, add ½ cup of the smoking chips to the fire in the kettle grill and place the meat on the rack over the drip pan. Cover the grill and cook 45 minutes, adjusting the vents to maintain the temperature. Remove the cover and transfer a couple of the glowing coals from the smaller grill to the fire. Add a small handful of smoking chips and quickly replace the cover. Continue replenishing the small grill with fresh briquets and adding burning briquets and smoking chips to the kettle grill every 45 to 60 minutes. Cook until the meat is quite tender, 6 to 8 hours in all. Check the water in the drip pan and replenish it as necessary with hot water. When done, the meat will still have a pinkish tinge, but it should register 160° to 165° on a meat thermometer.

4. Three to four hours before the meat is done, combine the vinegar and red pepper. If some of your guests are pepper-shy, hold back 2 tablespoons of the vinegar to use in place of the sauce for seasoning the meat before serving.

5. When the meat is done, remove it to a cutting board and cut or pull the meat away from the bones and skin. Shred the meat by hand, or chop it into small pieces. Place the meat on a serving dish, season it to taste with salt, and sprinkle it with a little of the barbecue sauce (or the reserved plain vinegar). Toast the buns on the grill and set out the platter of meat, coleslaw, and sauce for building and seasoning sandwiches to taste.

NOTE The seeds and pepper flakes can pack a real chile punch if they wind up in your sandwich. If you want to avoid this, strain the sauce after it has steeped for a few hours, or put it in a shaker bottle with a narrow spout that strains out the flakes as you pour.

TECHNIQUE NOTE The instructions in steps 1, 2, and 3 are for a charcoal grill. Of course, the cooking is much easier if you have a gas barbecue which can maintain the proper temperature. Smoking chips are essential with a gas grill for that true barbecued flavor; follow the manufacturer's instructions regarding when and where to add them.

Philadelphia Cheese Steak

Steak sandwiches never made sense to me until I tried this Philadelphia specialty. (How can you put a steak in a sandwich and bite through it easily?) Here the "steak" is very thin slices of beef which are cooked quickly on a griddle, along with onions and peppers. A slice of cheese is melted on top, and the whole drippy, gooey, delicious agglomeration is scooped onto a roll. Omit the cheese and you have a pepper steak, another popular sandwich.

Unless you have an electric slicer at home, it is difficult to slice the meat thinly enough. Ask the butcher to do it on his meat slicer. The slices should be as thin as possible without falling apart—"thin enough to read through," in the words of one Philadelphia native. Don't let the butcher try to sell you minute steaks, thicker cuts that have been run through a tenderizer. As they cook, they get their thickness back, and a thick piece of meat is all wrong here.

Serves 2

Olive or vegetable oil
½ medium onion, thinly sliced
1 medium sweet pepper, seeded and thinly sliced
½ pound eye of round, thinly sliced
Salt and pepper
2 to 4 slices mild cheddar or mozzarella cheese (enough to match the size of the rolls)
2 oval sandwich rolls, sliced and spread open

1. Have all the ingredients ready; this sandwich must be assembled quickly. Heat a large heavy skillet or griddle over medium-high heat. Moisten it with a little oil and cook the onion and pepper slices until soft and beginning to brown.

2. Push the onions and peppers aside and add the meat in one layer (you may need to do this in two batches). Cook the meat until browned on one side, turn it, season it with salt and pepper, and arrange the pieces in roughly the shape of the rolls. Immediately lay the cheese on top of the meat. Lay the open rolls face down over the meat and peppers. Continue cooking until the meat has lost its raw color, about 1 minute. Remove the rolls to a plate. Scoop the peppers and onions onto the meat and cheese, and transfer the whole mass with a spatula to the rolls. Serve immediately.

Croque Monsieur

This French grilled ham and cheese sandwich can be cooked in a skillet, in a special *croque monsieur* iron, or in a waffle iron that reverses to flat cooking plates (one that cooks both sides at once). Substitute cooked chicken breast for the ham and you have a *croque madame*. Gruyère is the traditional cheese for a *croque monsieur,* but any firm cheese that melts well will do. Try Dutch cheeses, Fontina or its many imitators, or a not-too-crumbly cheddar.

Serves 2

2 teaspoons butter (preferably unsalted)
4 slices whole wheat bread or good white bread
Mustard of your choice (optional)
3 ounces sliced flavorful ham (Black Forest, baked, or boiled)
2 ounces sliced Gruyère or other cheese

If using a *croque monsieur* iron, butter the inside of the iron and trim the bread to fit. Lay two slices of bread into one side of the iron and top them with mustard, ham, and cheese, then add the other two slices of bread. Close the iron and cook the sandwiches over medium heat, moving the iron around on the burner as necessary, until the sandwiches are golden brown on both sides and the edges are fused together. Serve warm.

If using a skillet or waffle iron, there is no need to trim the bread. Assemble the sandwiches and spread the butter on the outside of the bread. Cook the sandwiches until golden brown and crisp on both sides. Serve warm.

Soft-Shell Crab Sandwich

This sandwich is sure to get ooohs and ahhhs. After all, how often do you see a whole crab on a bun? When the blue crabs of the Atlantic and Gulf coasts shed their shells and set about growing new ones, they go through a soft-shell stage during which the whole crab is edible after the simplest cleaning. Look for them fresh in the spring and early summer, or frozen the rest of the year. In place of tartar sauce you can use your favorite dressing for fried shellfish—plain mayonnaise, a spicy Creole-style rémoulade sauce, or just a squeeze of lemon.

Serves 4

½ cup flour (approximately)
   Salt and freshly ground pepper
   OR Chesapeake Bay–style seafood seasoning
   Peanut or other vegetable oil
4 soft-shell crabs, fresh or thawed, cleaned
1 cup shredded lettuce
4 sesame-seeded hamburger buns, toasted
¼ cup tartar sauce or other dressing
   Lemon wedges

1. Put the flour in a shallow bowl and season it (lightly or liberally, as your taste dictates) with salt and pepper or seafood seasoning.

2. Fill a skillet with oil to a depth of ½ inch and heat it over medium-high heat until a pinch of flour foams instantly on hitting the oil. Reduce the heat to medium-low. Dredge the crabs in the seasoned flour, shaking off the excess, and cook as many as will fit in the oil at a time until golden brown, about 2 minutes per side. While the crabs are cooking, pile ¼ cup of shredded lettuce on the bottom half of each bun and top it with a tablespoon of tartar sauce. Drain the fried crabs briefly on paper towels and set them on top of the lettuce and sauce. Cover the buns and serve immediately, with lemon wedges on the side.

NOTE To clean soft-shell crabs, first cut across the front of the body with scissors or a knife to remove the eyes and mouth. Pull out the gray stomach sac. Carefully lift the corners of the shell and pull away the pointed, feathery gills underneath. Fold the corners back into place. The crab is now ready for cooking. If you buy live soft-shells, your fishmonger may clean them.

Zucchini Latkes on Dill Bread

Latkes are the savory pancakes of Eastern European Jewish cookery, of which the potato version is best known. No, I never heard of putting them in a sandwich either. But when I was thinking of vegetarian sandwiches, this idea popped up out of nowhere. It tastes great.

Serves 4

1 pound slender zucchini
   Salt
2 large eggs
3 tablespoons matzo meal or unsalted cracker crumbs
   Freshly ground black pepper
2 tablespoons (approximately) olive oil
8 slices Dill Bread (page 90) or other good white bread, toasted (see Note)
3 to 4 tablespoons plain yogurt or sour cream

1. Grate the zucchini on the coarsest side of a box grater or with the coarse disc of a food processor. Place the gratings in a colander, sprinkle them generously with salt, and let them stand 30 minutes to drain. Picking up a handful at a time, squeeze out as much moisture as possible.

2. Combine the zucchini, eggs, matzo meal, and pepper in a bowl to make a pancake batter. Heat a griddle or a couple of large, heavy skillets over medium heat and coat them well with oil. Make 4 large pancakes (the size of your bread). Cook them, turning them once, until well browned on both sides. Drain them on paper towels and place them immediately on 4 slices of toasted bread. Top each with yogurt or sour cream and a second slice of toast.

NOTE This sandwich tastes especially good on dill bread, but if you don't want to go to the trouble, just use a good white sandwich bread and add ½ teaspoon of dill weed to the zucchini mixture. Do toast the bread; for some reason untoasted bread tastes flat here.

Oyster Po' Boy

The po' boy, or oyster loaf, is one of two sandwiches for which New Orleans is famous. (The other is the Muffuletta on page 18.) The name po' boy has nothing to do with poor folks. It's derived from the French word *pourboire,* meaning a tip or a gift for services rendered, and is related to the sandwich's other nickname, "the peacemaker." According to local tradition, many a New Orleanian coming home after a night on the town has brought with him an oyster loaf as an appeasement for his spouse.

A real po' boy is made with deep-fried or pan-fried oysters stuffed inside a long hollowed-out loaf or sandwich roll. It's delicious that way, but I prefer this oven-fried version which eliminates the trouble of frying and shaves a few calories from the dish.

Serves 4

  1 cup yellow cornmeal or fine bread crumbs
¼ teaspoon salt
⅛ teaspoon each black and white pepper
    Pinch of cayenne
  1 loaf French bread (1–1½ pounds)
24 shucked oysters (about 1 pint—see Note), drained
    Vegetable oil
  3 tablespoons mayonnaise, with a little hot pepper sauce added if desired
  1 cup shredded lettuce

1. Preheat the oven to 400°. If your cornmeal is not especially finely ground, grind it in a food processor or blender for a minute or more. Combine the cornmeal and seasonings in a bowl. Split the bread open lengthwise and hollow out the top and bottom slightly (save the crumbs for another use). Open the loaf flat and toast it lightly in the oven.

2. Dredge the oysters in the cornmeal mixture, coating them all over, and arrange them on a lightly oiled baking sheet. Drizzle a tiny bit of oil over each oyster and bake them on the top shelf of the oven until golden brown, about 6 minutes. Pile the oysters into the loaf, spread the top half with mayonnaise, and add the lettuce. To serve, cut the sandwich crosswise into quarters.

NOTE Sizes and size grades of oysters differ in the East and West. If buying Atlantic or Gulf Coast oysters, choose selects (26 to 38 oysters per pint) or the slightly smaller standards (38 to 60 per pint). Pacific oysters generally run larger, so you can use fewer per serving. Smalls (the largest size I recommend) run 12 to 18 per pint; mediums run 10 to 12 per pint.

OPEN-FACE SANDWICHES

*Danish Smørrebrød
(recipes, page 58–61)*

Jean-Rodolphe's Sandwich

When I mentioned to my friend Pam that I was working on a sandwich book, she said, "You've got to include the wonderful grilled cheese sandwich that our host made for us in Lausanne, Switzerland." Here is how she described it. Dabbing the bread with a little wine is an unusual touch that helps tie all the flavors together. I have tried substituting Italian Fontina cheese for the Gruyère; it is equally delicious.

Serves 4

- 4 slices crusty white bread
- 1 ounce (approximately) dry white wine
  Dijon-style mustard
- 4 ounces sliced Gruyère cheese
- 1 medium tomato, scored and sliced
- ½ small onion, thinly sliced
  Freshly ground pepper to taste
  Fresh basil leaves (optional)

Toast the bread lightly on a grill or under a broiler. Moisten one side lightly with wine (your fingertips are the best tool for this). Spread on a thin layer of mustard, then add layers of cheese, tomato, and onion. Season generously with pepper. In summer, add some fresh basil leaves (torn into pieces if large). Return the sandwiches to the grill or broiler until the cheese is melted. Serve immediately.

Frangione a la Squid's

This exuberant, pizzalike sandwich was born at Augusta's restaurant in Berkeley, where I worked as a cook several years ago. Wendy Hallinan, the owner's daughter, came in one day with a recipe she had (literally) dreamed up. She had gone to bed with squid on her mind because she and her husband Danny were getting ready to open Squid's, their San Francisco restaurant dedicated to the tasty mollusc. The name *frangione,* by the way, means absolutely nothing; it was coined by one of the waiters and adopted because it sounded "really Italian."

Serves 3

- ⅓ to ½ pound sweet Italian sausage with fennel seeds
- 1 sweet or sour baguette (½ pound)
- ½ cup marinara sauce
- ¾ pound small squid, cleaned, sacs cut into
  ¼-inch rings (about 1 cup)
- 8 ounces sliced mozzarella cheese

1. Skin the sausages and break the meat into clumps. Brown the meat slowly in a skillet until fully cooked and crumbly. Drain.

2. Preheat the oven to 400°. Split the baguette lengthwise, open it out flat, and cut it crosswise into thirds. Spread the bread with a thin layer of marinara sauce. Scatter the crumbled sausage over the sauce, add an even layer of squid, and top with the cheese. Bake 12 minutes or until the cheese is thoroughly melted and beginning to brown and the squid in the center feels firm when touched with a fork. Serve open face, to be eaten with knife and fork.

Bruschetta

In central and southern Italy, various toasted or grilled breads are referred to as *bruschetta*. At its simplest, topped with just olive oil and garlic, bruschetta is the original garlic bread. Other traditional versions include tomatoes, cheese, herbs, or other seasonings. Less tradition-bound cooks have taken the idea beyond its origins, as the following two examples show.

Since bruschetta is mostly bread, be sure to use a good bread. The crusty white bread described on page 5 is just right, or use something with a small amount of whole grain flour mixed in. Darker, more grainy-tasting breads can be too heavy or too strong in flavor for this treatment.

Ideally, bruschetta should be cooked over an open fire. It's an ideal appetizer when you are grilling outdoors; just toast a few slices of bread on the edge of the fire before or as the main dish cooks and add the desired toppings. You can even toast the bread in a fireplace, impaled on long forks or on a special fireplace grill. An oven broiler also works fine.

Bruschetta with Peaches and Fresh Cheese

Karen Lucas and Lisa Wilson, two talented young chefs now in the catering business in Oakland, California, generously provided this recipe for an unusual sweet-savory bruschetta. Try it as an appetizer for a summertime dinner, or along with a salad for lunch.

Serves 4

> 1 cup Fresh Homemade Cheese (see below)
> OR 1 cup ricotta cheese blended with
> 2 tablespoons orange juice
> 1 ripe but firm peach, sliced
> 4 large, thick slices crusty white bread
> Pinch of salt

Have the cheese and peach at room temperature. Grill or broil the bread until lightly browned on both sides. Spread the cheese on the warm bread, sprinkle with salt, and arrange the peaches on top. Serve immediately.

Fresh Homemade Cheese

Makes 1 cup

> 1 quart milk
> ⅔ cup half-and-half
> Juice of 2 oranges and 2 lemons

Heat the milk and half-and-half to just below boiling in a nonaluminum saucepan; remove from the heat. Strain the citrus juice into the milk. Let the mixture stand until the milk is thoroughly curdled, about 15 minutes. Gently pour the mixture into a large sieve lined with cheesecloth, letting the liquid drain off into a bowl or sink. Gather the ends of the cheesecloth around the curds and tie the cloth into a bundle which can be hung from a faucet. Let the bundle drip into the sink for at least an hour, or until firm. Remove the cheese from the cloth, wrap it well, and store it in the refrigerator for up to 4 days.

Bruschetta di Prosciutto e Funghi (Prosciutto and Mushroom Toasts)

To appreciate this autumnal treat you must make it with genuine Italian Fontina, preferably Fontina Val d'Aosta. No other cheese has exactly the same flavor and perfect melting texture. It marries beautifully with the taste of mushrooms and ham. For an even more glorious combination, try using fresh *porcini* mushrooms *(Boletus edulis)*, which grow wild over much of the country in fall and early winter and are increasingly available commercially.

Serves 4 for lunch, 6 to 8 as an appetizer

- ¼ **pound large fresh mushrooms**
- 1 **teaspoon clarified butter or neutral vegetable oil**
- 1 **baguette, split and cut into quarters,**
  OR **4 large slices crusty white bread**
- 1 **ounce prosciutto, thinly sliced and cut into noodle-size shreds**
- 4 **ounces Italian Fontina cheese, sliced**

1. Clean the mushrooms with a brush or a slightly damp towel (avoid washing them if possible). Cut them vertically into ¼-inch-thick slices. If using fresh *porcini*, slice the stems thinner than the caps. Heat a skillet over high heat, add the oil or butter, and quickly cook the mushrooms until they begin to exude their liquid. Reduce the heat to medium and continue cooking until the liquid is nearly evaporated. Transfer the mushrooms to a shallow bowl. If you wish, let the mushrooms cool and continue making the bruschetta later.

2. Broil the bread slices lightly on one side. Turn them over and cover the uncooked side with a layer of mushrooms. Scatter prosciutto over the mushrooms and top them with a layer of cheese. Return the sandwiches to the oven and broil until the cheese melts.

VARIATION To prepare bruschetta on an outdoor grill, assemble the toppings on the raw bread, then toast the sandwiches near the edge of the fire until the cheese is melted. Use a cover if your grill has one.

VARIATION To make the sandwich with dried *porcini*, cover ½ ounce of the dried pieces with lukewarm water and let them soak for 1 hour. Lift the pieces out of the water, dice them finely, and return them to the water to wash away as much dirt as possible. Lift the pieces out again. Saute them in the butter along with ½ cup minced onion. Carefully pour a tablespoon or two of the clear soaking liquid into the skillet, leaving the dirt behind, and cook until the mixture is nearly dry. Spread it on the toasted bread and continue the recipe as described above.

Asparagus Cheese Toast

This sandwich and a bowl of soup was one of my family's favorite weekend lunches when I was growing up. Canned asparagus may not be fashionable today, but I think they're excellent for this purpose—maybe even better than fresh.

Serves 4

- 1 **large, firm but ripe tomato**
- 8 **small or 4 large slices rye bread, preferably seedless**
  Mustard of your choice
- 1 **can (15 ounces) asparagus spears, well drained**
  OR **1 pound thick asparagus spears, cooked until tender**
- 8 **small or 4 large slices cheese (about 4 ounces): Swedish or Danish Fontina, sharp cheddar, or domestic Muenster**

1. Score the tomato with 4 or 5 very shallow cuts through the skin from top to bottom, then cut it crosswise into thin slices. Toast the bread lightly on one side if desired.

2. Spread the untoasted side of the bread lightly with mustard. Top each slice with a layer of asparagus, a layer of tomato, and a slice of cheese cut as closely as possible to the shape of the bread. Broil until the cheese melts and begins to brown, 2 to 3 minutes. Serve warm.

Smørrebrød (Danish Open-Face Sandwiches)

One of the best-known specialties of Denmark is *smørrebrød*, an assortment of open-face sandwiches eaten with a knife and fork. Living in an extremely cold climate, Danes eat a high-fat diet; being predominantly a dairy country, they get most of their fat from butter and cream. *Smør* is the Danish word for butter, and the bread in authentic Danish *smørrebrød* is liberally smeared with butter before the other toppings are added. Living as I do in California, I keep the butter layer on my *smørrebrød* thin, and I recommend that you do the same.

In Denmark, simple *smørrebrød* are eaten frequently at home, sometimes as a first course or a light lunch, and more elaborate versions are served at parties and special dinners. My wife lived on a small Danish mink farm one summer and remembers plates of bread, butter, pâté, and various cheeses often on the table for do-it-yourself *smørrebrød*. In a fine restaurant on Midsummer's Eve, the platter set before her held *smørrebrød* topped with, among other delicacies, breast of squab and smoked eel.

A *smørrebrød* platter makes a delightful casual meal. The sandwich toppings can be varied endlessly. Cold cooked shrimp on a lettuce leaf, "Italian salad" (finely cut cooked vegetables in mayonnaise), and leftover cooked meats are all appropriate toppings. Serve an assortment of several different *smørrebrød* on one or more platters, figuring you will need six small sandwiches for each person.

Remember to choose the combinations of bread and topping carefully; the bread must be sturdy enough in flavor and texture to support the topping, both literally and figuratively. In general, darker meats and stronger-flavored toppings should go on pumpernickel or other dark, strong breads, while fish and delicate cheeses call for lighter breads; but there are exceptions. A sample selection of *smørrebrød* follows. Serve the sandwiches with a good Danish beer or, if you want to be really festive, with shots of ice-cold *akvavit* and beer chasers. (To get *akvavit* as cold as it should be, wrap the bottle in a wet towel and put it in the freezer until the towel freezes. Serve straight from the freezer, in shot glasses.)

Egg and Anchovy Smørrebrød

When looking for flavors to dress up hard-boiled eggs, I always come back to anchovies. It's a recurring theme, from Scandinavia to the south of France (think of salade niçoise) to all-American deviled eggs.

Makes 2 sandwiches

1 or 2 canned anchovy filets, drained and rinsed
1 tablespoon softened unsalted butter
2 thin slices fine white bread
2 hard-boiled eggs, sliced
Chopped chives and slivers of red pepper, for garnish

Chop the anchovies as finely as possible and stir them into the butter. Spread the bread slices with anchovy butter and top them with egg slices. Sprinkle the tops with chopped chives and garnish with red pepper slivers.

Dill Havarti Smørrebrød

A *smørrebrød* platter should include at least one cheese sandwich; here is one suggestion. Blue cheese (often topped, like steak tartare, with a raw egg yolk) is another traditional favorite. Also try caraway-flavored Dutch or domestic Kuminost.

Makes 2 sandwiches

2 slices pumpernickel, spread with unsalted butter
2 ounces sliced Havarti cheese with dill
4 cornichons

Cover each slice of bread with overlapping slices of cheese. Cut the cornichons into fan shapes by making 3 or 4 parallel cuts in each one, from one end almost to the other. Fan two cornichons out on each sandwich.

Smørrebrød. On plate: Egg and Anchovy (left), Liver Pâté and Cucumber. On boards, clockwise from top: Steak Tartare, Pickled Herring and Beet, Dill Havarti

Smoked Fish and Potato Smørrebrød

This sandwich can be made with any hot-smoked fish, including trout, whitefish, herring, sturgeon, and tuna. Fine cold-smoked salmon deserves a plainer treatment—just serve it on buttered whole wheat bread with a sprinkling of chopped dill.

Makes 2 sandwiches

> 2 thin slices fine white bread, spread with unsalted butter
> 1 small red potato, steamed or boiled and thinly sliced (see Note)
> 1½ ounces smoked fish, in ⅛-inch-thick slices
> 1 teaspoon sour cream
> ½ teaspoon cream-style horseradish
> Small sprigs of fresh dill

Top each slice of bread with a layer of overlapping potato slices, then a layer of fish. Combine the sour cream and horseradish and put a dollop in the center of each sandwich. Garnish with a few sprigs of dill.

NOTE To slice a cooked potato with minimal damage to the skin, use your thinnest, sharpest paring knife and dip it in water between slices.

Steak Tartare Smørrebrød

A whole egg yolk is the traditional topping for this mixture of chopped raw beef and onions, but the yolks of typical American large eggs seem too big. Try it with small or medium eggs; for an even more delicate touch, I use quail eggs. Any time you are going to eat raw meat, make certain it is perfectly fresh; buy the steak from a butcher you trust.

Makes 2 sandwiches

> 6 ounces beef steak (loin or sirloin)
> 2 tablespoons minced raw onion
> 2 slices dark pumpernickel, spread with unsalted butter
> 2 quail egg yolks
> 1 teaspoon capers
> Freshly ground black pepper

Trim off all visible fat from the steak and chop the meat as finely as possible with a chef's knife, or scrape the meat repeatedly with the edge of the knife until only the sinews remain. Combine the chopped or scraped meat with 1 tablespoon of onion and spread the mixture on the bread slices, heaping it slightly in the middle. Make a depression in the center of each portion with a small spoon and drop a raw egg yolk into it. Garnish the meat with capers and the remaining onion and sprinkle the top with pepper.

Liver Pâté and Cucumber Smørrebrød

Liver pâté is commonly made at home in Denmark, but you might find it more convenient to buy a prepared version in a delicatessen. There are also some very good canned liver pâtés; or you could use Jewish-style chopped chicken liver.

Makes 2 sandwiches

> 2 slices dark pumpernickel or crispbread, spread with unsalted butter
> 2 ounces liver pâté, fresh or canned
> ½ small cucumber (preferably the slender, nearly seedless English or Japanese variety)
> Thinly sliced radishes, for garnish

Spread each slice of bread with an even layer of pâté. Make cucumber curls by trimming a peeled section of cucumber to a rectangular shape, then pulling off long, thin sheets with a vegetable peeler. Top each sandwich with two rows of cucumber curls, curled side up and overlapped like shingles. Top each cucumber curl with a slice of radish.

Pickled Herring and Beet Smørrebrød

If you can stand to get yet another variety of bread for *smørrebrød,* this sandwich works best on a lighter style of pumpernickel. Sometimes called Bavarian style, it is between ordinary rye bread and a true dark, sour pumpernickel. Otherwise, use the dark variety.

Makes 2 sandwiches

¼ cup thinly sliced red onion rings
  Water
1 teaspoon vinegar
  Pinch of salt
2 slices medium pumpernickel, spread with unsalted butter
½ cup (approximately) boiled or pickled beets, well drained
3 ounces pickled herring, well drained

1. Place the onion rings in a small bowl and cover them with water. Add the vinegar and salt and let the bowl stand 30 minutes.

2. Top the bread with a layer of sliced beets. Bone the herring pieces or slice them crosswise into pieces less than ½ inch thick. Arrange them on top of the beets. Drain the onion rings and scatter them on top.

STUFFED AND ROLLED SANDWICHES

Greek Salad Sandwich
(recipe, page 69)

Roast Beef Lavash Roll with Horseradish

This is the most basic type of lavash roll sandwich. The possibilities for variations are endless. Once you are comfortable with the procedure, try putting your own combination of tender meats, cheeses, spreads, or any other fillings you like into the roll.

Serves 3 to 4

> 1 large round lavash (⅓ pound)
> 1½ teaspoons cream-style horseradish
> 2 tablespoons mayonnaise
> ⅓ pound thinly sliced roast beef
> 2 medium tomatoes, sliced as thin as possible
> 3 or 4 outer leaves of romaine, center ribs removed

1. Dampen one large or two smaller kitchen towels (enough to cover both sides of the lavash) and wring out the excess moisture. Moisten the lavash well on both sides under cold running water. Place it darker side down between layers of damp towel and set it aside until soft and pliable, about 45 minutes. The dampened lavash can sit for several hours after softening.

2. Remove the top towel. Trim the edges of the lavash slightly to produce an approximately square sheet about 12 inches across. Combine the horseradish and mayonnaise and spread it thinly over the surface from the near edge to within 2 inches of the far edge. Spread the roast beef in an even layer over the horseradish and top it with a layer of tomatoes. If the tomatoes are not sliced thin enough to cover the whole sheet, arrange them in an even band across the middle. Lay the romaine leaves on top; stop about 4 inches from the far edge (the leaves will slide somewhat in rolling).

3. Using the towel to help lift the sheet, fold an inch or so of the near edge over the filling, then gently but firmly roll up the entire sheet jelly-roll fashion. Wrap and chill the sandwich until ready to serve, 1 to 24 hours. To serve, trim the edges and, using a thin knife, cut the roll crosswise into ¾-inch slices.

Smoked Salmon Lavash Roll

Smoked salmon and cream cheese, the perennial favorites to accompany bagels, also make a perfect filling for a rolled sandwich. A bit of fresh dill, a traditional flavor partner to salmon, adds an attractive green color to the spiral of white and pink.

Serves 3 to 4

> 1 large round lavash (⅓ pound)
> 6 ounces cream cheese (regular or whipped)
> 1 tablespoon milk
> 1 tablespoon chopped fresh dill
> Pinch of salt
> 1 teaspoon Dijon-style mustard (optional)
> ¼ pound cold-smoked salmon, thinly sliced (see Note)
> Freshly ground black pepper to taste

1. Dampen one large or two smaller kitchen towels (enough to cover both sides of the lavash) and wring out the excess moisture. Moisten the lavash well on both sides under cold running water. Place it darker side down between layers of damp towel and set it aside until soft and pliable, about 45 minutes. The dampened lavash can sit for several hours after softening.

2. Combine the cream cheese and milk in an electric mixer (or use a bowl and a wire whisk) and beat until quite light. Remove half and set it aside. In a mortar, crush the dill with a pinch of salt until it exudes a lot of green juice. Mix the contents of the mortar into half of the cream cheese.

3. Remove the top towel from the lavash. Trim the edges slightly to produce an approximately square sheet about 12 inches across. Spread the plain cream cheese over the near half of the sheet, spreading it evenly to the edges. Top the cheese with a thin layer of mustard, if desired. Spread the green cream cheese on the other half of the sheet, again being sure to go all the way to the edges. Arrange the salmon slices in a single layer, beginning 1 inch from the near edge and extending an inch or two beyond the middle of the sheet.

$\longrightarrow$

4. Using the towel to help lift the sheet, fold the near edge an inch or so over the salmon, then roll up the entire sheet jelly-roll fashion. Roll gently but firmly—the idea is to avoid pockets of air in the roll, but not to squeeze the filling out as you go.

5. The roll can be sliced right away, but it is easier to handle if wrapped and chilled for an hour or more, or even overnight. Trim the edges and, using a thin knife, cut the roll crosswise into ¾-inch slices. Top each slice with a little freshly ground pepper.

NOTE Be sure to use cold-smoked salmon, otherwise known as lox or nova. This type is not cooked in the smoking process, which keeps it soft enough to slice thinly. Hot-smoked salmon, sometimes called kippered, is fully cooked and is too crumbly to slice thinly.

Turkey and Cranberry Roulade

These colorful pinwheel sandwiches are a new twist on a favorite combination, turkey and cranberry. Thinly sliced turkey, cranberry sauce, spiced mayonnaise, and lettuce are all spread on a rectangle of tender white bread, then rolled up like a jelly roll and sliced. The same filling also works well as a conventional sandwich, on whole wheat or white bread. Either way, it's a soft sandwich, so serve some crunchy pickles or crudités alongside.

Serves 4

　1　teaspoon caraway seeds
　¼　cup mayonnaise, bottled or homemade (see page 95)
　¼　teaspoon turmeric
　½　cup whole cranberry sauce, canned or homemade
　1　loaf Egg Bread (page 87) baked in a loaf pan
　　　OR 1 loaf Basic White Bread (page 84)
　　　or other good white bread, unsliced
　　　Tender lettuce leaves, such as butter or oak leaf
　½ to ¾ pound thinly sliced turkey breast

1. Crush the caraway seeds in a mortar or mince them as finely as possible with a knife. Combine them with the mayonnaise and turmeric and refrigerate the mixture for at least 2 hours to allow the flavors to develop. Strain the cranberry sauce through a coarse sieve, pressing hard to get all the pulp through while straining out the skins.

2. With a bread knife or other long, sharp knife, trim the bottom crust off the loaf of bread. Set the loaf cut side down on a cutting board. With the knife held horizontally, cut a ¼- to ⅜-inch-thick slice off the bottom. Remove the slice and repeat three times, making four large rectangular slices. Trim off the crusts.

3. Lay the bread slices on the board with the short sides toward you. Spread each slice with the seasoned mayonnaise. Add a layer of lettuce, stopping 1 inch from the far end. Top the lettuce with a layer of turkey, also leaving 1 inch at the end, then spread the turkey with the strained cranberry sauce. Gently roll the bread up around the filling jelly-roll fashion, making four thick cylinders, each about 4 inches long. Wrap each sandwich in plastic wrap and set it aside for 30 minutes at room temperature.

4. Just before serving, unwrap the rolls and slice each into thirds. Secure the loose ends with toothpicks if necessary.

Stuffed Pita Sandwiches

The round, flat bread known as pita is a favorite all around the eastern Mediterranean. Cut in half or slit open along one edge, it becomes a pocket to be stuffed with fillings; left whole, it can be rolled around a stuffing like a very thick tortilla. It's a versatile bread that has found its way into mainstream American kitchens, where it has been known to hold everything from traditional Middle Eastern fillings to turkey, avocado, and alfalfa sprouts.

Two of the following pita sandwiches are Mediterranean favorites, one Greek and one Arabic. The other two are less authentic, but I think equally delicious. One is derived from the classic Greek summertime salad of tomatoes, feta cheese, and olives; the other contains seasoned meatballs or *keftas,* which in various versions (and spellings) are eaten from Morocco and Greece to India.

There is really no limit to what you can stuff inside a pita or roll a pita around. Try sliced meats, cooked and shredded chicken, cheeses, fried tofu or tempeh, or any of the taco and burrito fillings on page 77–78. From there, just use your imagination!

Keftas in Pita

You can vary the flavor of these meatballs by drawing on the various seasonings of the Middle East, North Africa, and India, where they are popular. Indian *garam masala* (mixed hot and sweet spices) can take the place of the ground spices. Parsley or cilantro can substitute for the mint. A teaspoon of minced fresh ginger in place of the ground ginger will give tiny nuggets of ginger flavor. Although lamb is the most common meat for keftas, beef, veal, ground turkey, or even pork—whatever you would use for a meat loaf—will do.

Serves 4

½ **pound boneless lamb (not too lean)** OR **ground lamb**
¼ **cup minced onion**
8 **large leaves fresh mint**
½ **teaspoon ground coriander**
¼ **teaspoon ground ginger**
⅛ **teaspoon ground cumin**
  Pinch of ground cloves
  Pinch of salt
  Olive oil
1 **cup diced tomato**
2 **tablespoons chopped fresh mint**
½ **cup plain yogurt or Tzatziki Sauce (page 69)**
4 **pitas, halved and opened into pockets**

1. Cut the lamb into 1-inch cubes and combine it in a food processor with the onion, mint leaves, spices, and salt; chop finely. If you don't have a food processor, use ground lamb; chop it again with the onions and mint, transfer it to a bowl, stir in the spices and salt, and beat with a spoon until the mixture smears against the side of the bowl.

2. Heat a skillet and add just enough oil to coat the surface. Cook a pinch of the lamb mixture, taste it for seasoning, and correct if necessary. With moistened hands, make 2 dozen small meatballs and cook them in the skillet over low heat until done to your taste, 4 to 6 minutes. Covering the pan loosely will cut down on splattering.

3. Toss the tomatoes and chopped mint together and set them out in a bowl. Set the yogurt or Tzatziki out in another bowl. For each sandwich, drop 2 or 3 meatballs into a pita half and add tomatoes and yogurt to taste.

Greek Salad Sandwich

When perfectly ripe tomatoes are in season, they deserve center stage. In Greece, where some of the world's best tomatoes grow, they are often combined with cucumbers, tangy feta cheese, black olives, fruity olive oil, and oregano in a salad. It may be unconventional to stuff a salad inside a pita, but it makes a memorable summer sandwich.

Serves 4

- 1 pound ripe but firm tomatoes, scored and sliced
- 1 small cucumber, peeled and thinly sliced
- 1 tablespoon extra-virgin olive oil
- ½ teaspoon dried Greek oregano
  Freshly ground pepper to taste
- 4 pitas, halved and opened into pockets
- ½ pound feta cheese (Bulgarian, Greek, or Corsican), sliced or crumbled
  Kalamata or other black olives, for garnish

1.   Arrange the tomatoes and cucumbers in a shallow bowl, overlapping them slightly. Drizzle them with the oil and scatter oregano and pepper over them. Let them stand 30 minutes.

2.   Slip the tomato and cucumber slices into the pita pockets, add the cheese, and spoon a little of the liquid from the tomato bowl into each. Serve with plenty of olives on the side.

Souvlaki Pita

I will never forget the *souvlaki pita* I tasted at a little store-front shop in Chania, Crete. The vendor sliced small chunks of lamb off a vertical spit-roaster *(gyro)* and rolled them in a warm pita along with sliced onions that had been browning in the drippings below the spit. He topped it off with chunks of perfectly ripe tomato and the incomparable thick Greek yogurt. It was heavenly.

   This is not the authentic Greek souvlaki-stand method, but then, few home kitchens have a *gyro* (or the crowds to feed from it). Cooking the meat in a skillet then browning the onions in the drippings gives nearly the same flavor to just a few servings.

Souvlaki Pita

Serves 4

- 2 lamb shoulder chops, about ½ pound each
  Salt and pepper
- 1 medium onion, halved and thickly sliced
- 4 pitas
- 1 cup diced tomato
- 1 recipe Tzatziki Sauce (below) or ½ cup plain yogurt

1.   Heat a skillet or griddle over medium-high heat. Add the lamb chops and cook, turning once, until done to taste, about 5 minutes per side for medium rare. Season after turning with salt and pepper.

2.   Remove the chops to a cutting board and scatter the onion slices in the skillet. Lay one or two of the pitas concave side down on top of the onions to steam for a minute or so. Meanwhile, cut the meat from the chops, trim off the outer fat, and slice the meat into thin, bite-size strips. When the pitas have softened, remove them and add the other two.

3.   For each sandwich, lay a quarter of the chopped meat onto a pita; add some onions, tomatoes, and yogurt. Roll the pita around the filling, pinching one end closed as much as possible. Wrap the closed end in foil or heavy waxed paper to make the sandwich easier to hold. Serve immediately.

Tzatziki Sauce

Made with larger pieces of cucumber, garlicky *tzatziki* is a common side dish or appetizer in Greek meals. In this form, it becomes a pungent sauce for cooked lamb.

Makes about ¾ cup

- ½ cup peeled, seeded, and finely diced cucumber (about ½ of a medium cucumber)
- 1 small clove garlic, minced
  Pinch of salt
- ¼ cup plain yogurt

Combine all the ingredients and let the mixture stand at least 1 hour, preferably longer. Refrigerate if not used within 2 hours. The sauce will keep for a day in the refrigerator, but the garlic flavor may get unpleasantly strong.

Felafel

Throughout the Arab world, street vendors sell fried balls of ground and seasoned chickpeas *(felafel)* stuffed into pita pockets and topped with a creamy or spicy sauce. In Israel, felafel is a popular street food among Jews and Arabs alike, so much so that it has been called "the Israeli hot dog."

As long as you remember to soak the chickpeas ahead of time, it takes just a few minutes to whip up a felafel mixture. If you are really in a hurry, some health food and international food stores sell dry instant felafel mixes that reconstitute with water in a few minutes. Brands vary from quite good to horrible, so shop around.

Serves 4

> 1 cup (⅓ pound) dried chickpeas
> ½ cup chopped onion
> 2 cloves garlic
> 1 tablespoon fresh coriander (cilantro)
>   or parsley leaves
> ½ teaspoon salt
> ½ teaspoon ground coriander
> 1 teaspoon ground cumin
> ⅛ teaspoon freshly ground black pepper
> ⅛ teaspoon cayenne (or more or less to taste)
>   Pinch of turmeric
> 1 cup (approximately) olive or vegetable oil
> 4 pitas, halved and opened into pockets
>   Tahini Sauce (right)
>   Spicy Tomato Relish (right)
>   OR ½ cup diced fresh tomatoes
> ½ cup shredded lettuce

1. Soak the chickpeas overnight in 3 cups of water; drain. Grind the chickpeas with the onion and garlic in a meat grinder or food processor. Stir in the remaining seasonings and let the mixture stand 15 to 30 minutes. (Cover and refrigerate for longer storage, up to 24 hours.)

2. With a measuring spoon and moistened hands, scoop a heaping tablespoon of the mixture into your palm and shape it into a patty about ½ inch thick. Make 8 patties in all. Heat a skillet and add oil to a depth of ¼ inch. Fry the patties over medium heat until golden brown on both sides; drain them on paper towels. For each sandwich, tuck 2 patties inside a pita pocket, add either Tahini Sauce or Tomato Relish or both, and garnish with lettuce.

Tahini Sauce

Tahini is richer than its light flavor might suggest. It's more than half oil, and the rest is mostly protein, so a little of this sauce goes a long way.

Makes ½ cup

> 2 tablespoons tahini (sesame seed paste, available
>   in health food stores and Middle Eastern markets)
> 1 clove garlic, minced
> ¼ teaspoon salt
>   Pinch of cayenne
> 1 to 2 teaspoons lemon juice
> ¼ cup plain yogurt

Combine the tahini, garlic, salt, cayenne, and 1 tablespoon of the lemon juice in a bowl and beat with a spoon or whisk until smooth. Stir in the yogurt, taste for seasoning, and correct if necessary with more salt or lemon juice. To prepare in a blender or food processor, simply combine all the ingredients and blend until smooth.

Spicy Tomato Relish

The considerable fire in this relish comes from a dab of very potent bottled chile paste. Among the types that work well are Chinese or Vietnamese chile paste with garlic, Indonesian *sambal ulek,* and Moroccan *harissa.* If fresh red chiles are more easily available, just mince one and sprinkle it with a little salt to draw out its juices.

Makes about ½ cup

> 1 medium tomato, finely diced
> 1 clove garlic, minced
> 1 tablespoon lemon juice
>   Pinch of sugar
> ¼ teaspoon chile paste

Combine all the ingredients and let the mixture stand 15 minutes or so for the flavors to blend.

Mu Shu Pork

Mu shu pork consists of a savory stir-fry of shredded pork and vegetables that is rolled into thin Mandarin pancakes and eaten with the fingers. Actually, proper Chinese etiquette dictates that you use a combination of fingers and chopsticks to roll the pancake around the filling and use chopsticks to hold the closed end of the roll while eating.

Because the shape of the cut ingredients is so important in Chinese cooking, I have gone into some detail discussing the cutting of each ingredient. To make other mu shu dishes, substitute beef, chicken, turkey, or cakes of fried tofu for the pork.

Serves 4

- 3 scallions (green onions), trimmed
- 1-inch section fresh ginger
- 1 medium carrot
- ¼ cup sliced bamboo shoots
- ½ pound boneless pork loin
- 1 tablespoon soy sauce
- 2 tablespoons water
- Pinch of sugar
- 3 tablespoons peanut or other vegetable oil
- 2 eggs, lightly beaten
- ¼ cup cloud ear mushrooms (see Note), soaked in warm water and drained
- 8 to 10 Chinese pancakes (see Note), warmed in a steamer or on a dry skillet
- ¼ cup hoisin sauce

1. Separate the green scallion tops and white bottoms. Cut the white parts into 1½-inch sections, split them lengthwise, and cut them lengthwise into shreds. Cut the green tops into shreds in a similar fashion and set them aside. Peel the ginger and cut it crosswise into thin slices; stack the slices and cut them into tiny sticks. Combine the ginger slices with the white scallion shreds.

2. Cut the carrot on a diagonal to make about ¼ cup of oval slices about 1½ inches long; stack these and cut them lengthwise into sticks. Cut the bamboo shoots into similar sticks. Slice the pork across the grain into ⅛-inch-thick slices; trim the slices to 1½ inches long, stack them, and slice them

into shreds a little wider than ⅛ inch. Arrange all the cut ingredients on a plate. Combine the soy sauce, water, and sugar in a small bowl and set it aside.

3. Heat a wok or a large skillet over medium heat. Add 1 tablespoon of oil and swirl the pan to coat the sides. Add the eggs and cook just until they set, forming a thin omelette. Remove the omelette to the cutting board and cut it into thin noodlelike shreds.

4. Wipe the pan clean, turn the heat to high, and add the remaining oil. When the oil is hot, add the ginger and scallion, stir-fry a few seconds until fragrant, and add the pork. Cook just until the meat loses its raw color. Add the carrots, bamboo shoots, and cloud ears and stir-fry 2 minutes longer. Add the soy sauce mixture and the egg strips and cook until nearly all the liquid is evaporated. Taste for seasoning, correct it if necessary, and transfer the stir-fry to a serving dish.

5. Serve the warm pancakes on a separate plate; set the scallion tops and hoisin sauce out in small dishes. For each serving, spread a pancake with a little hoisin sauce, add a few scallion shreds, and top with some pork mixture. Roll the pancake around the filling, fold one end over and pinch it shut, and eat with the fingers.

NOTE Cloud ears are a type of dried mushroom found in Chinese markets in small cellophane packages, sometimes labeled "black fungus" or simply "dehydrated vegetable." The pieces are typically less than an inch long and nearly black; when rehydrated they swell to several times that size. Don't confuse them with the larger and tougher wood ears, which are noticeably two-toned. Chinese (Mandarin) pancakes or *bao bing* are very thin rounds of wheat dough, usually found in the refrigerator or freezer section of Chinese markets. Round Philippine *lumpia* wrappers, or even small flour tortillas, will do as a substitute.

Tacos and Burritos

In any city where there is a Mexican-American population, you will find *taquerías* selling two of Mexico's favorite street foods, tacos and burritos. The crisp-fried fast-food taco filled with crumbly ground beef, familiar throughout the United States, is almost unknown in Mexico. A true Mexican taco is a soft corn tortilla, or sometimes two, wrapped around a savory filling. The filling may be as simple as some *carnitas* (chunks of lightly browned braised pork), *carne asada* (thinly sliced and grilled beef steak), or boiled beef tongue with a few cubes of fresh tomato. Or it may be a more elaborately seasoned meat, such as *chilorio* (pork braised with chiles, spices, and vinegar) or chicken simmered with green chiles and onions. Some versions also include beans, but that is pushing the limits of a typical 6-inch tortilla.

Replace the corn tortilla with a flour tortilla and the taco becomes a burrito. Flour tortillas are the favorite snack bread of northern Mexico, which is wheat country. Since many of the Mexican immigrants in this country come from the north, burritos are especially popular here. Another probable reason for their popularity is that you can pack much more filling into a burrito than a taco. At least in California, taquerías seem to compete to see who can come up with the most enormous "super burrito." Some stuff a single flour tortilla with what must be a pound or more of rice, beans, meat, lettuce, salsa, sour cream, and guacamole. Even the regular burrito typically contains rice, beans, and salsa in addition to meat.

Both tacos and burritos lend themselves to easy, do-it-yourself entertaining, indoors or out. Just lay out the ingredients — warm tortillas in a napkin-lined basket, fillings and garnishes in separate bowls — and let diners build their own creations.

Burritos

Serves 4

> 4 extra-large flour tortillas
> (10 to 12 inches in diameter)
> 1 cup well-seasoned cooked beans, drained
> 1 cup cooked rice (long or short grain, white or brown)
> 1 cup filling (pages 77–78)
> Fresh Tomato Salsa (page 96) to taste
> OR 1 peeled, seeded, and chopped tomato
> plus Dried Chile Salsa (page 96) to taste

Heat the tortillas one at a time on a dry skillet until pliable or, better yet, warm them in a steamer which will hold them flat. (A Chinese bamboo steamer, though hardly authentic Mexican cookware, is ideal for steaming tortillas.) Spread a spoonful of beans in a rectangle in the center of each tortilla; top with a spoonful of rice, the filling of your choice, and salsa. Fold the tortilla over both ends of the rectangle, fold one remaining side over the filling, then roll the whole package over, enclosing the filling. Wrap each burrito in foil, if desired, to keep it warm and help enclose the filling; peel away the foil as you eat.

Burrito filled with Carnitas
(page 77)

Soft Tacos

Serves 4

8 6-inch corn tortillas
1 cup cooked pinto or black turtle beans,
    well drained
1 cup filling (right)
    Fresh or bottled tomato salsa to taste
    OR 1 peeled, seeded, and chopped tomato
    plus Dried Chile Salsa (page 96) to taste
½ cup shredded lettuce

Heat the tortillas one at a time on a dry skillet or griddle until pliable. Top each tortilla with a spoonful of beans, then filling, then your choice of salsa. Top with a bit of lettuce. Fold the tortilla up around the filling. Pinch one end shut while you bite into the other.

VARIATION To have more room for more filling, some taquerías use two overlapped tortillas for each taco. I prefer to use the tortillas separately and have two smaller tacos.

TACO AND BURRITO FILLINGS

Carnitas (Braised and Browned Pork)

Carnitas ("little meats") are chunks of pork cooked by an ingenious and, as far as I know, uniquely Mexican method. They are simmered in water until tender, then the water is allowed to evaporate until the meat begins to brown in its own rendered fat. The result is a marvelous interplay of textures—tender inside, lightly crisp outside, and not at all greasy.

Makes 3 cups

1½ pounds boneless pork shoulder (yield from
    a 2¾ pound piece with skin and bone)
    Water

1. Trim most of the visible fat from the meat and cut it along the natural seams into chunks no more than 2 inches thick. Remove any tough outer membranes from the muscles. Place the meat in a deep, heavy pot and add cold water to cover. Bring the water to a boil, reduce the heat to maintain a lively simmer, and cook uncovered until the meat is tender, about 2 hours. Skim off any foam that rises to the surface during cooking.

2. When the meat is tender, raise the heat slightly so the water cooks away more rapidly (but keep it below a rolling boil). Continue cooking until the meat begins to sizzle, showing that the water is gone and the meat is cooking in its rendered fat. Let it brown and get slightly crisp on all sides. Drain it and keep it warm until ready to serve, then pull it into shreds or chop it into bite-size chunks.

NOTE This recipe makes enough for about a dozen servings. Store leftover meat tightly wrapped in the refrigerator or freezer. To reheat, wrap it in foil and warm it in a steamer or in a low oven.

Soft Tacos filled with Chilorio
(page 78)

Chilorio
(Spiced Braised Pork)

Cooking carnitas with chiles and vinegar was originally a way of preserving the meat. This spicier version will last longer in the refrigerator than unseasoned carnitas. Because there is plenty of chile flavor here, use a plain tomato and onion salsa for garnish, not one with additional chiles.

Makes 3 cups

1½ pounds boneless pork shoulder
 4 dried ancho chiles
 4 cloves garlic
 ¼ teaspoon peppercorns
 ⅛ teaspoon cumin seeds
 ¼ teaspoon oregano
 ⅓ cup mild vinegar (Japanese rice or apple cider)
 ¼ cup water
 1 teaspoon salt
   Pinch of ground cloves

1. Cook the meat as for Carnitas (page 77) up to the point where the liquid has evaporated and the meat begins to sizzle. Meanwhile, heat an ungreased skillet or griddle over low heat and toast the chiles until they become warm and pliable (do not let them blacken). Remove them and set them aside to cool. Toast the whole garlic cloves in the skillet until fragrant. Peel them and put them in a blender or mini-chopper. Toast the peppercorns, cumin seeds, and oregano for just a few seconds and add them to the blender.

2. Slit or tear the chiles open; discard the stems, seeds, and ribs. Tear the chiles into small pieces. Add them to the blender and grind until no large pieces remain. Add the vinegar, water, salt, and cloves and blend to a coarse paste.

3. Shred the cubes of meat. An easy way to do this is to place the cubes one at a time on a cutting board and whack them with the side of a cleaver, breaking the meat into strings which barely hold together. Transfer the contents of the blender to the pot in which the meat was cooked and cook it for a minute or so over low heat. Stir in the shredded meat and cook slowly until nearly dry. Keep the meat warm until ready to serve, or wrap and store it, as for Carnitas.

Pollo con Rajas y Crema
(Chicken with Green Chiles and Cream)

Cream is used a lot in Mexican cooking, often (as here) to help carry and soften the flavor of hot chiles. Don't worry too much about the added calories; most of it gets left behind in the pot.

Makes about 2 cups

1½ to 2 pounds chicken parts
   Water or unsalted chicken stock
 1 tablespoon oil or chicken fat
 1 large onion, split vertically and sliced
 4 large green chiles (poblano, pasilla, Anaheim, or New Mexico) roasted and peeled and cut into narrow strips (see Rajas under Quesadilla Fillings, page 81)
 ½ cup sour cream or whipping cream
   Salt to taste

1. Place the chicken parts in a heavy pot just large enough to hold them snugly. Add water or stock to cover. Bring just to a boil, reduce to a simmer, and skim off any foam that rises to the surface. Simmer until the chicken is quite tender, 45 minutes to 1 hour. When the chicken has simmered for 30 minutes, heat the oil (or a little chicken fat skimmed from the pot) in a small skillet over low heat. Add the onion. Cook gently until it softens, then add the chile strips and cream. Simmer 15 minutes.

2. Remove the cooked chicken from the broth and pull the meat from the bones (discard the skin if desired). Pull the meat into large shreds with your fingers or two forks. Add the chicken to the pan with the chiles and cream; stir to moisten it evenly. Add salt to taste and keep warm until ready to serve. To use in tacos or burritos, lift the meat and vegetables out of the sauce with a slotted spoon; drain them well so just a bit of the cream clings to the meat.

Quesadillas

Quesadillas (from the Spanish *queso,* cheese) might be called Mexican grilled cheese sandwiches. In northern Mexico they are made with flour tortillas, which are topped with a cheese filling, cooked on a griddle until the cheese melts, and folded in half. In central and southern Mexico, quesadillas are more likely to be thick cheese-filled turnovers, made from a raw dough like that used for corn tortillas and either toasted on a griddle or fried.

The best cheese for quesadillas is one that melts easily without separating and becomes slightly stringy when pulled apart. Mexican markets in some areas sell local versions of Mexican cheeses, of which Asadero ("the grilling one") is ideal. Otherwise, high-moisture Jack and domestic Muenster are the closest to Mexican cheese in cooking qualities. Mild or medium cheddars also work, but sharp aged cheddars tend to separate, spilling butterfat out the ends of the quesadilla. Experiment with other cheeses that you like.

Corn Quesadilla

Makes 8 (serves 2 to 4)

- 1 cup *masa harina* (specially prepared corn flour for tortillas)
- ½ cup (approximately) lukewarm water
- ½ cup grated cheese
- ½ cup quesadilla filling (optional; see page 81)

1. Combine the *masa* and water and stir well until the mixture forms a thick, evenly moistened dough. Pinch off enough dough to make a 1¼-inch ball. Roll the ball between your palms until smooth, then place it between layers of wax paper or plastic wrap. With a tortilla press or a rolling pin flatten it into a 5-inch circle.

2. Heat a well-seasoned griddle or one or two large skillets over medium heat. Peel the top piece of wax paper off a circle of dough. Turn it over into your hand and peel off the second piece of paper. Turn the circle of dough over onto the griddle.

3. Immediately spread a tablespoon of cheese over the middle of the circle. Lay a heaping tablespoon of filling across one side and fold the other side over with a spatula to form a semicircle. Press the edges of the semicircle together with your fingertips. Cook the quesadilla on both sides until well browned, about 1½ minutes per side. Continue with the remaining dough and filling as space becomes available on the griddle. Serve immediately, or keep warm in a 200° oven for a few minutes before serving.

Flour Quesadilla

Serves 1

1 large flour tortilla
1 ounce sliced or grated cheese
1 to 2 teaspoons Fresh Tomato Salsa (page 96),
    well drained, or bottled chunky tomato and chile
    salsa
1 tablespoon quesadilla filling (optional; see below)

Warm the tortilla on an ungreased griddle or in a large skillet until pliable. Arrange the cheese on one side of the circle leaving a ½-inch rim around the edge. Top the cheese with salsa and/or a filling and fold the unfilled side of the tortilla over. Cook, turning once, until both sides are lightly browned and crisp.

QUESADILLA FILLINGS

RAJAS (Roasted and Peeled Chile Strips)   Roast 1 or 2 whole large green or red chiles over a gas flame or under a broiler, turning them so the skin blisters evenly all over. Close the roasted chiles in a large jar, covered bowl, or paper bag so that they steam from their own heat. When cool, peel away the skins and slit the chiles open lengthwise. Remove the stems, seeds, and veins and cut the chiles into long strips. One large chile makes enough *rajas* for 4 flour or 8 corn quesadillas. *Note:* The dark green, pointed *chile poblano* is the most popular for *rajas* in Mexico; it varies from medium to quite hot. The more slender green Anaheim variety is both milder and more commonly available. Any large sweet or hot pepper—red, green, yellow, or purple—can be roasted the same way.

SQUASH OR PUMPKIN BLOSSOMS Remove the stems and fuzzy sepals from 6 blossoms; chop the remaining parts coarsely and saute them in a little oil with 2 tablespoons of minced onion until wilted. Makes ½ cup.

LEFTOVER COOKED CHICKEN, TURKEY, OR DUCK Cut the meat into strips or, better yet, pull it into coarse shreds by hand.

CANNED TUNA (believe it or not) For flour quesadillas only. As this tends to be a little drippy, I recommend a different folding method. Place the cheese down the middle of the warmed tortilla, starting a couple of inches in from one side. As soon as it begins to melt, place 2 to 3 tablespoons of drained tuna and a dollop of salsa on top. Fold the near edge of the tortilla over the filling, then fold in the two sides, making an open-topped envelope. By the time you have finished filling and folding, the package should be ready to turn and toast briefly on the other side. My 3-year-old daughter calls these "tuna pockets."

Flour Quesadillas filled with Pollo con Rajas y Crema
(page 78)

BREADS AND SPREADS

Yeasted Walnut Bread (recipe, page 89)
spread with mustard
Top left: Fresh Tomato Salsa (recipe, page 96)
Bottom left: Mayonnaise with herbs (recipe, page 95)

Basic White Bread

A tender white bread with a good crust should be in every sandwich maker's repertoire. This basic loaf cuts easily, toasts well, and has a clean, not-too-sweet taste. Best of all, it's pretty easy to make, even for beginning bakers.

Makes 2 loaves

- ¼ cup warm (100°) water
- 2 teaspoons (1 envelope) active dry yeast
- 2 cups milk
- 1 tablespoon sugar
- 2 teaspoons salt
- 1 tablespoon unsalted butter
- 5½ to 6½ cups all-purpose flour

1. Put the water in a small bowl and sprinkle the yeast over it. Stir and let it stand until the yeast softens. Meanwhile, scald the milk (see step 1, page 92). Stir in the sugar, salt, and butter and let the mixture cool about 7 minutes.

2. Transfer the milk mixture to a large mixing bowl and stir 3 cups of the flour into it. Add the softened yeast and beat with a wooden spoon to a smooth batter, about 100 strokes. Add 2 more cups of flour, ½ cup at a time, and stir until the mixture becomes too thick to stir by hand. Turn the dough and any unincorporated flour out onto a well-floured surface. Knead the dough, adding flour as needed to keep it from sticking to the board, until it is smooth, springy, and no longer sticky, about 7 to 9 minutes.

3. Wash and dry the bowl, oil it lightly, and return the ball of dough to it. Turn the dough over once to coat it lightly with oil. Cover the bowl with a dry towel and let the dough rise until doubled in bulk, about 1 hour. Punch it down and let it rise again until doubled, about 45 minutes.

4. Punch the dough down and divide it in half. Form each half into a loaf; place the loaves in two greased loaf pans. Cover the pans with a towel and let the loaves rise to slightly above the tops of the pans, about 45 minutes.

5. Preheat the oven to 400°. Bake the bread in the middle of the oven until it is nicely browned and the loaves sound hollow when tapped on the bottom, about 35 minutes. (Lift a loaf from the pan with a pot holder to test it.) Remove the loaves from the pans immediately and let them cool on a rack. Let the bread cool thoroughly before slicing.

Basic Whole Wheat Bread

I usually bake my own whole wheat bread, because it's nearly impossible to find a commercial version that is not overly sweet. This bread, hearty but not heavy, proves you don't need any sweetener at all to make a good whole wheat bread. What you do need is a little more time for the dough to develop than in some other breads. The sponge method is the key; it gives the yeast time to work on plain flour without the inhibiting effect of salt and oil, and results in a lighter dough.

Makes 2 loaves

2½ cups warm (100°) water
2 teaspoons (1 envelope) active dry yeast
2½ cups whole wheat flour
¼ cup vegetable oil
2½ teaspoons kosher salt
3 to 3½ cups unbleached all-purpose flour or bread flour

1. Run hot water in a large bowl to warm it. Empty the bowl and add the measured warm water. Sprinkle the yeast over the water and let the bowl stand until the yeast sinks.

2. Add the whole wheat flour and stir with a wooden spoon to make a thick batter. Beat the batter 100 strokes with the spoon, then lay a clean, dry dish towel over the bowl and set it in a warm place (75° to 85°) for 1 hour. When the mixture has risen by at least a third and is full of air bubbles, it is a sponge.

3. Stir the oil and salt into the sponge, deflating it to a thick batter again. Add unbleached all-purpose flour a cup at a time until the dough is too thick to stir with the spoon. Spread about a cup of all-purpose flour on a work surface and dump the dough out onto it. Knead the dough until smooth and elastic, adding more flour to the table as long as the dough keeps absorbing it. When done, the dough will no longer feel sticky and an indentation made with a finger will rise slowly back.

4. Wash the sponge bowl with warm water and dry it thoroughly. Oil the bowl. Put in the dough and turn it once so that it is covered with a film of oil. Put a dry towel over the bowl and set it back in the warm place. Let the dough rise until doubled in bulk, about 50 minutes. Punch it down and let it rise another 40 minutes.

5. Divide the dough in half. Form each half into a loaf and place the loaves in two greased loaf pans. Cover the pans with the towel and let the loaves rise to slightly above the tops of the pans, about 20 minutes.

6. Preheat the oven to 350°. Bake the bread in the middle of the oven for 1 hour. (To test for doneness, tap on the bottom of a loaf; it should sound hollow.) Remove the loaves from the pans immediately and let them cool on a rack. Let the bread cool thoroughly before slicing.

TECHNIQUE NOTE If you don't have time to make the bread in one stretch, you can refrigerate the dough at various stages to slow down the process for your convenience. For example, you can make the sponge in the morning and refrigerate it, then remove it from the refrigerator when you get home from work, knead in the rest of the flour, and have freshly baked bread by bedtime. Or refrigerate the dough after kneading and let it undergo its first rising overnight in the refrigerator. Use plastic wrap rather than a towel to cover the bowl for refrigerator storage.

Pane all'Olio
(Olive Oil Bread)

This is one of my favorite sandwich breads; the recipe was inspired by the breads I ate in Italy. It can be made entirely with white flour, but a small amount of whole wheat flour gives a fuller, earthier flavor without much affecting the texture. The oblong loaf provides uniform slices of a convenient size for sandwiches. The Italians call a loaf of this shape a *mantovana;* the French call it a *bâtard.*

Makes 2 loaves

2¼ **cups warm (100°) water**
1½ **teaspoons active dry yeast**
¾ **cup whole wheat flour**
4 **cups bread flour or unbleached all-purpose flour**
2 **heaping teaspoons kosher salt**
   OR 1¼ **teaspoons table salt**
¼ **cup fruity olive oil**

1. Put the water in a large mixing bowl and sprinkle the yeast over it. When the yeast sinks (after 3 to 5 minutes) add the whole wheat flour and 1½ cups of the bread flour. Beat with a wooden spoon to a smooth batter, about 100 strokes. Cover the bowl with plastic wrap and set it aside in a warm place (70-80°) for 1 hour. The mixture, called a sponge, should rise a couple of inches and become quite bubbly.

2. Sprinkle the salt over the surface of the sponge and pour in the oil; stir until well incorporated. Add 2 cups of bread flour and stir until the mixture becomes too thick and sticky to stir by hand. Turn the dough out onto a floured surface. With lightly oiled hands pull all the bits of dough out of the bowl. Knead the dough, adding flour as needed to keep it from sticking to the board, until it is smooth, cohesive, springy, and no longer sticky, about 7 to 10 minutes.

3. Wash and dry the bowl, oil it lightly, and return the ball of dough to it. Turn the dough over once to coat it lightly with oil. Cover the bowl and let the dough rise until doubled in bulk, about 50 minutes. Punch it down and let it rise again until doubled, about 40 minutes.

4. Line the bottom rack of your oven with unglazed quarry

tiles or a pizza stone, move the other rack as high as possible, and preheat the oven to 375°. Punch down the dough, divide it in half, and form each half into an oblong loaf about 10 inches long. Keep the sides of the loaves as straight as possible from end to end, so the slices will be of uniform size. Set each loaf on one end of a lightly floured kitchen towel (not terry cloth) and fold the towel over to loosely cover it. Let the loaves rise 20 minutes. While they are rising, set a shallow pan of water on the high oven shelf.

5. Sprinkle a baker's peel or an upside-down cookie sheet with cornmeal. Roll one loaf, still wrapped in its towel, over onto its top, then use the towel to invert it onto the peel. Handle it gently so as not to deform it or knock the air out. With a very sharp knife make a single lengthwise slash in the top nearly the length of the loaf or make two or three diagonal slashes. Swab the hot tiles with a wet rag held in a long pair of tongs, or spray them with water from a spray bottle. Place the tip of the peel near the back of the tiles and, with a quick jerk, pull the peel out, sliding the loaf off of it onto the tiles. Repeat with the second loaf, placing it beside the first on the tiles. Bake the loaves until the bottoms sound hollow when thumped, about 45 minutes. Transfer them to a wire rack and let them cool thoroughly before slicing or wrapping.

TECHNIQUE NOTE Although baking tiles are not essential for this kind of loaf, I recommend them highly. Baking on a porous surface gives bread an especially crunchy bottom crust (and makes incomparable pizza). Cookware stores sell specially designed pizza stones, but 6-inch square unglazed quarry tiles (sold in building supply stores and tile shops) are cheaper. Four to six of them should suffice to cover your oven rack.

If your stone or arrangement of tiles is not big enough to accommodate both loaves (allowing room for expansion during baking), divide the dough in half after kneading and place the halves in separate bowls. Cover and refrigerate one bowl while the dough in the other undergoes its first rise, then take it out. The chilling will delay the rising just long enough that the second loaf will be ready to bake when the first one comes out of the oven. Check the water level in the pan on the top shelf before baking the second loaf and add more if necessary.

Lacking tiles, you can bake the loaves on sheet pans and still come out with an excellent bread. Let the loaves rise on the pans, then bake them on the bottom shelf of the oven.

Egg Bread

Like Jewish challah and French brioche, this fine-textured white bread gets extra richness and flavor from the addition of eggs. It's a fine all-purpose white sandwich bread, and is perfect for tea sandwiches and Turkey and Cranberry Roulade (page 66).

Makes 2 loaves

2 cups warm (100°) water
2 teaspoons (1 envelope) active dry yeast
2 tablespoons sugar
2 teaspoons salt
2 large eggs, at room temperature
3 tablespoons plus 1 teaspoon oil or melted butter
6½ to 7 cups unbleached all-purpose flour
   or bread flour

1. Place the warm water in a medium bowl and sprinkle the yeast over it. Let it stand until the yeast dissolves and sinks. Add the sugar, salt, eggs, and 3 tablespoons of oil and stir until well combined.

2. Measure 5 cups of the flour into another, larger bowl. Make a well in the center and pour in the liquid ingredients. Stir until the flour is incorporated and forms a thick batter. Add another ½ cup of flour and stir until the mixture becomes too thick to work with a spoon. Scrape the dough out onto a well-floured surface and knead, adding flour as necessary to keep the dough from sticking, until it is smooth, resilient, and only slightly sticky, 6 to 8 minutes. Wash and dry the bowl and rub it with 1 teaspoon of oil. Return the dough to the bowl; turn it once to coat it with oil. Cover the bowl with plastic wrap and let the dough rise until doubled in bulk, 45 minutes to an hour.

3. Punch the dough down and let it rise again until doubled, about 40 minutes. Preheat the oven to 350°. Punch the dough down again. Divide it in half and form each half into a loaf, stretching the top surface so that it is smooth but not torn; tuck the sides and ends under. Grease two loaf pans (or coat them with nonstick spray) and place the loaves in them, seam side down. Cover the pans loosely and let the dough rise until it reaches the top of the pans. Bake on the middle shelf of the oven for 1 hour, or until the loaves sound hollow when thumped on the bottom (they should slide out of the pans easily for testing). Remove the loaves from the pans promptly and cool them on a wire rack.

TECHNIQUE NOTE To bring refrigerated eggs to room temperature in a hurry, place them in a small bowl and cover them with hot tap water. They will be ready in 5 to 10 minutes.

Focaccia
(Italian Flat Bread)

Focaccia is similar to Pane all'Olio (Olive Oil Bread, page 86) but it is even richer in oil. The original Italian focaccia was baked directly on a stone hearth, producing a round, crusty bread shaped like a thick pizza. When given a long time to rise and baked on a sheet pan, it comes out a soft, uniform rectangle, perfect for splitting for sandwiches.

Makes 1 sheet (11 × 17 inches)

> 2 cups warm (100°) water
> 1 heaping teaspoon active dry yeast
> 4 to 4½ cups bread flour or unbleached
>   all-purpose flour
> 2½ teaspoons kosher salt OR 1½ teaspoons table salt
> ¼ cup plus 1 tablespoon fruity olive oil
> 2 teaspoons fresh rosemary leaves or chopped
>   fresh sage or basil (optional)

1. Put the water in a large mixing bowl and sprinkle the yeast over it. When the yeast sinks (after 3 to 5 minutes) stir in 2 cups of the flour. Beat with a wooden spoon to a smooth batter, about 100 strokes. Cover the bowl with plastic wrap and set it aside in a warm place (70–80°) for 1 hour. The mixture, called a sponge, should rise a couple of inches and become quite bubbly.

2. Sprinkle the salt over the surface of the sponge and pour in ¼ cup of the oil; stir until well incorporated. Add 1½ cups of flour and stir until the mixture becomes too thick and sticky to stir by hand. Turn the dough out onto a floured surface. With lightly oiled hands pull all the bits of dough out of the bowl. Knead the dough, adding flour as needed to keep it from sticking to the board, until it is smooth, cohesive, and slightly sticky, about 7 to 10 minutes.

3. Wash and dry the bowl, oil it lightly, and return the ball of dough to it. Turn the dough over once to coat it lightly with oil. Cover the bowl and let the dough rise until doubled in bulk, about 50 minutes.

4. Punch down the dough and gently stretch it by hand into a rectangle roughly the size of your cookie sheet. Use a rolling pin only if necessary to keep the dough from tearing. Gently press the rectangle into the cookie sheet, stretching here and pushing together there to get it all the way into the corners and make the thickness as even as possible. Cover the sheet with plastic wrap and let the dough rise in a warm place until doubled in thickness, about 2 hours; or put the sheet in a cool place and let the dough rise overnight.

5. Preheat the oven to 400°. Dimple the top of the bread all over with your fingertips, making shallow indentations every inch or so. Brush the surface with the remaining oil and sprinkle it with herbs if desired. Bake on the upper shelf of the oven for 20 minutes, rotating the pan halfway through baking. Let the bread cool in the pan.

Yeasted Walnut Bread

This bread is a close cousin to Pane all'Olio (page 86); it has a mild nut oil in place of the olive oil and chopped walnuts are kneaded in. I developed it for the blue cheese and pear sandwich on page 23, but try it in any sandwich where you feel the flavor of walnuts would add to the overall effect. Leg of Lamb Sandwich with Roasted Garlic (page 20) is a good candidate.

Makes 2 loaves

2¼　cups warm (100°) water
1½　teaspoons active dry yeast
¾　cup whole wheat flour
4　cups bread flour or unbleached all-purpose flour
2　heaping teaspoons kosher salt
　　OR 1¼ teaspoons table salt
¼　cup peanut or walnut oil (the cold-pressed type sold in health food stores, not the imported variety)
1　cup walnut halves or pieces, chopped
　　Cornmeal

1. Put the water in a large mixing bowl and sprinkle the yeast over it. When the yeast sinks (in 3 to 5 minutes) add the whole wheat flour and 1½ cups of the bread flour. Beat with a wooden spoon to a smooth batter, about 100 strokes. Cover the bowl with plastic wrap and set it aside in a warm place (70-80°) for 1 hour. The resulting sponge should rise a couple of inches and be quite bubbly.

2. Sprinkle the salt over the sponge and pour in the oil. Stir until well incorporated, then add 2 cups of bread flour. Stir until the mixture becomes too thick and sticky to stir by hand. Turn the dough out onto a floured surface, and with lightly oiled hands pull all the bits of dough out of the bowl. Knead the dough, adding flour as needed to keep it from sticking to the board, until it is smooth, cohesive, springy, and no longer sticky, about 7 to 10 minutes. When the dough is almost done, scatter the chopped nuts over the surface and knead them in.

3. Clean the bowl and oil it lightly. Return the ball of dough to the bowl, turning it over once to coat it lightly with oil. Cover the bowl and let the dough rise until doubled in bulk, about 50 minutes. Punch it down and let it rise again until doubled, about 40 minutes.

4. Line the bottom shelf of the oven with unglazed quarry tiles or a pizza stone. Position the other oven rack as high as possible and preheat the oven to 375°. Punch down the dough, divide it in half, and form it into 2 round balls, stretching the top of the dough gently and tucking the edges under. Set each loaf on one side of a lightly floured kitchen towel (woven, not terry) and loosely cover it with the other side. Let the loaves rise 20 minutes.

5. While the loaves are rising, set a shallow pan of water on the uppermost shelf of the oven. Sprinkle a baker's peel or an upside-down cookie sheet with cornmeal. Roll the loaves, still wrapped in their towels, over onto their tops. Use the towel to invert the first loaf onto the peel. With a very sharp knife, slash a 4-inch square on top. Swab the hot tiles with a wet rag held in a long pair of tongs, or spray them with water from a spray bottle. Place the tip of the peel near the back of the tiles and, with a quick jerk, pull the peel out, sliding the loaf onto the tiles. Repeat with the second loaf. Bake the breads until the bottom crusts sound hollow when thumped, about 45 minutes. Transfer the loaves to a wire rack and let them cool thoroughly before slicing or wrapping.

TECHNIQUE NOTE If your baking tiles are not big enough to accommodate both loaves at once, see the Technique Note under Pane all'Olio (page 86).

Quick Nut Bread

This is a dense, slightly sweet bread perfect for tea sandwiches or as a base for mild cheeses. Half the nuts are ground and added to the flour so that their flavor suffuses the entire bread; the rest are chopped to provide nuggets of both flavor and texture.

Makes 1 loaf

- ½ cup nuts (walnut or pecan halves and pieces or whole hazelnuts [filberts])
- 1½ cups all-purpose flour
- 1½ teaspoons baking powder
- ¾ teaspoon salt
- 4 tablespoons unsalted butter, softened
- ¼ cup sugar
- 1 large egg
- 2 tablespoons honey
- ¾ cup milk
- 1 teaspoon vanilla extract

1. Preheat the oven to 350°. Have all the ingredients at room temperature. Lightly grease an 8 × 5-inch or smaller bread pan; dust it with flour, shaking out the excess.

2. Grind half the nuts. A hand-held rotary grater does this well and quickly; otherwise, use a food processor or blender, chopping with a pulsing action. Chop the remaining nuts by hand into pieces no larger than ¼ inch.

3. Combine the flour, ground nuts, baking powder, and salt and stir until well blended. In another bowl, cream the butter and sugar together (with a wooden spoon, a hand-held mixer, or a tabletop mixer) until very light and fluffy. Add the egg and beat just until combined. Stir in the honey, milk, and vanilla. Add the flour mixture and chopped nuts and stir just until the flour is evenly moistened (do not overmix or the bread will be tough and will have tunnels).

4. Scrape the batter into the loaf pan and spread it evenly. Bake it on the middle shelf of the oven until a thin knife or skewer inserted into the center comes out clean, about 50 minutes. Let the bread cool 15 minutes in the pan on a cooling rack, then loosen it with a knife and turn it out onto the rack. When cool, wrap in foil and store at room temperature.

Dill Bread

I don't know who first thought to combine dill and cottage cheese in a bread, but I do know it was a stroke of genius. The resulting loaf, called dilly bread in some quarters, is moist, springy, and very tasty. This recipe makes one small loaf, enough for about 8 sandwiches.

Makes 1 loaf

- ¼ cup warm (100°) water
- 2 teaspoons (1 envelope) active dry yeast
- 1 cup large curd cottage cheese (see Note)
- 4 teaspoons sugar
- 1 small green onion, chopped
- 1 tablespoon unsalted butter, soft
- 1 teaspoon salt
- 1 large egg
- 2 to 2½ cups all-purpose flour
- 1 tablespoon chopped fresh dill
  - OR 2 teaspoons dried dill

1. Put the water in a small bowl and sprinkle the yeast over it. Stir and let it stand until the yeast softens (3 to 5 minutes). Meanwhile, heat the cheese in a small saucepan until it is just warm to the touch. Transfer it to a large bowl and stir in the sugar, onion, butter, and salt. Beat the egg and stir it in. Stir in ½ cup of flour and then the softened yeast and the dill.

2. Add flour ¼ cup at a time, beating well after each addition, until you have a very stiff batter. Cover the bowl with a dry towel and set it in a warm place. Let the batter rise until double in bulk, about 1 hour. Stir the batter until deflated and fairly smooth; it will be quite sticky. Spread it in a small (5-by 8-inch) greased bread pan. Cover it with a towel and allow it to rise until it reaches the top of the pan, about 45 minutes.

3. Preheat the oven to 350°. Bake the bread in the middle of the oven until the crust is deep brown and the bottom sounds hollow when tapped, 45 to 50 minutes (lift the loaf up with a pot holder to test it). Turn the loaf out of the pan immediately and let it cool completely on a wire rack before slicing.

NOTE Do not substitute small curd or low-fat cottage cheese. They become gummy during the mixing process and can spoil the texture of the bread. I don't know why.

Lavash
(Armenian Cracker Bread)

This bread is traditionally baked in large rounds, but unless you have a couple of large pizza pans, it's easier to bake in rectangles. Use the largest cookie sheets or jelly-roll pans you have. An 11 × 14-inch rectangle is equal in size to a 14-inch circle—and it's a better shape for rolling sandwiches. To use homemade sheets in place of the round ones, arrange the filling ingredients on the moistened bread, leaving a 1-inch border along both short ends. Fold the near border over the filling and roll the bread up into an 11-inch-long log.

Makes 4 sheets (about 1¼ pounds)

- ⅔ cup milk
- ½ cup cold tap water
- 1 teaspoon active dry yeast
- 4 cups unbleached all-purpose flour
- 1½ teaspoons sugar
- 1½ teaspoons salt
- ¼ cup vegetable shortening
- 1 heaping tablespoon sesame seeds

1. Scald the milk. (To scald, bring the milk almost to a boil in a small saucepan; remove it from the heat when a ring of bubbles appears around the edges.) Combine the scalded milk and the water in a bowl. Let them cool to about 100°, then sprinkle on the yeast. Let the bowl stand until the yeast sinks and dissolves.

2. Meanwhile, combine the flour, sugar, and salt in a large mixing bowl. Add the shortening and cut it into the flour with the paddle attachment of an electric mixer, a hand-held mixer, or a pastry blender, or by rubbing the flour and shortening between your fingertips. Continue until no visible lumps of shortening remain. Switch to a dough hook if using a tabletop mixer.

3. Pour the yeast mixture into the flour; be sure to scrape in all the yeast from the bottom of the bowl. Mix the dough at medium-low speed until it comes together, then knead it until smooth, another minute or so. If mixing by hand, stir with a wooden spoon until the dough becomes too stiff to work,

then turn it out onto a lightly floured surface and knead it until smooth. Divide the dough into quarters and roll each quarter into a smooth ball. Wrap each ball loosely in plastic wrap and set them aside to rest for 10 to 30 minutes.

4. Preheat the oven to 400°. Position one oven rack as high as possible in the oven and the other in the middle. Place a shallow pan containing an inch of hot water on the top shelf. On your work surface assemble two large (11 × 17-inch) greased sheet pans, a rolling pin, a spray bottle of water or a wide pastry brush, and flour for dusting.

5. Flatten a ball of dough into a circle on a lightly floured surface and roll it into a rectangle measuring about 11 by 14 inches. Don't worry if the edges are a little irregular, but try to get the thickness as even as possible. Transfer the sheet to a baking pan. Bake it on the middle shelf of the oven for 4 minutes. While it bakes, roll out the next sheet of dough.

6. After 4 minutes, remove the first pan and place the second in the oven. Puncture and deflate any large bubbles in the first bread and invert it. Spray or brush the top with water to moisten it lightly. Scatter a quarter of the sesame seeds over the top. When the second sheet has baked for 4 minutes, remove it and return the first one to the oven. Bake it until lightly browned on top and crisp, another 4 to 5 minutes. Meanwhile, invert, moisten, and seed the second sheet.

7. Remove the breads from the pans after the second baking and cool them on a wire rack. Let the pans cool, then repeat steps 5 and 6 with the remaining pieces of dough. Let the breads cool completely, then stack and store them in a large plastic bag. They will keep up to one week.

Pita
(Middle Eastern Pocket Bread)

Perhaps surprisingly, perhaps not, this bread can be made with the same dough as lavash. In commercial bakeries, it's baked right on the brick floor of an oven, as it has been for thousands of years. Here is a method that replaces the direct heat of the oven bricks with a quick turn in a skillet before baking.

Makes 8 breads

⅔ **cup milk**
½ **cup cold tap water**
1 **teaspoon active dry yeast**
4 **cups unbleached all-purpose flour**
1½ **teaspoons sugar**
1½ **teaspoons salt**
¼ **cup vegetable shortening**

1. Prepare Lavash dough (page 92) through step 3, but divide the dough into 8 even pieces instead of 4. (A scale is useful for dividing the dough evenly.) Set the balls of dough on a lightly floured sheet pan, covered with a towel. Preheat the oven to 400°; position one rack in the middle of the oven, the other near the top.

2. Heat a griddle or 2 heavy skillets over medium heat until a drop of water dances on the surface for a few seconds before evaporating. Roll 2 balls of dough into 6½-inch circles. (Keep the others covered with the towel to prevent drying.) Toast each circle on the griddle for 15 seconds per side—no longer (see Technique Note). Transfer the circles immediately to a cookie sheet and bake them on the middle shelf of the oven until puffy and lightly browned, about 4 minutes (see Note). Meanwhile, roll out the next 2 pieces of dough and prepare to toast them and bake them on a second cookie sheet.

3. When the first breads have baked 4 minutes, turn them over and move the sheet to the top shelf; bake until the breads are lightly browned, 1 to 2 more minutes. Add the new pan

to the middle shelf and bake as above. Repeat with the remaining balls of dough.

4. After baking, wrap the breads in kitchen towels to cool. They will gradually deflate. When thoroughly cool, place them in one or two plastic bags. Pita are best on the day they are baked or the next day, but they will keep up to 4 days.

TECHNIQUE NOTE Do not toast the breads in the skillet any longer than 15 seconds per side or the crusts will be too thick and the bread won't puff.

NOTE Some of the breads may not puff up in the oven, or may puff unevenly. Leave them in to bake a minute or two longer, then wrap them and let them cool with the others. Once cool, they can usually be cut in half and the sides carefully separated to form a pocket. Of course, if you are using them unsplit as for Souvlaki Pita (see page 69), it doesn't matter if they puff up or not.

VARIATION For a heartier flavor, replace 1 cup of the unbleached flour with whole wheat flour.

Homemade Nut Butters

Once you have made your own nut butters, you may never settle for plain peanut butter again. Each nut gives its own special character to a spread. Cashew butter is sweet, luscious, and altogether nutty. Almond butter has a deeper, subtler, but more substantial flavor. Hazelnut butter gets a distinctive and strong flavor from the skins of the nuts—too strong a flavor for some.

Makes ½ cup

> 1 cup shelled nuts—cashew halves and pieces, blanched whole almonds, or hazelnuts (filberts)
> 1 to 3 teaspoons peanut oil, if needed
> Salt to taste

1. Toast the nuts in the oven or in a skillet until slightly browned. To toast in an oven, spread the nuts in a single layer in a shallow pan and bake at 350° for 10 minutes, stirring the nuts occasionally so they brown evenly. To toast on top of the stove, place the nuts in a skillet and cook them over medium-high heat, stirring or shaking the pan constantly so they brown evenly. Be sure that you turn all the nuts over frequently as they cook or they will scorch. A teaspoonful of oil helps distribute the heat and keep everything moving, resulting in more even browning.

2. Transfer the toasted nuts to a food processor and process 1 minute. Stop the machine, scrape the sides and bottom of the bowl thoroughly, and continue processing another minute or two, scraping the bowl occasionally. Eventually the sound will change as the mixture changes from finely chopped nuts to a thick, smooth mixture that clings to the sides of the bowl. Have patience; this can take two or three minutes. If the nuts refuse to form a butter, add a little oil through the feed tube (hazelnuts usually require some oil). When the blade spins free, scrape down the mixture one more time and blend a few seconds more. Taste the butter and add a little salt if desired; process briefly to stir it in. Store nut butters tightly covered, at room temperature or refrigerated, and use within a week or so.

Tapenade

Tapenade is an endlessly variable spread made from black (fully ripe) olives. Most versions include garlic and anchovy; some substitute tuna for the anchovy; some include capers or herbs. However you make it, it's a delicious spread for crackers or sliced bread as well as a condiment for sandwiches, fish, or meats. It is used in the swordfish sandwich on page 30, but I wouldn't blame you if you just spread a thin layer of it on bread and called it a sandwich. It keeps well, so keep some on hand in the refrigerator for an instant hors d'oeuvre.

Makes a scant ½ cup

> ½ cup (3 ounces) whole brine-cured black olives
> 2 anchovy filets, rinsed and chopped
> 2 cloves garlic, minced
> 2 tablespoons fruity olive oil
> 1 teaspoon lemon juice, or to taste
> Freshly ground pepper to taste

Crush the olives against a cutting board with the side of a broad knife blade and remove the pits. Add the anchovies and garlic to the pile of olives and chop everything together to a coarse paste. Transfer the mixture to a bowl, beat in the oil, and season to taste with lemon juice and pepper. Store in a tightly sealed jar in the refrigerator for up to 2 weeks.

VARIATION If you prefer a smoother texture, or you want to make tapenade in quantity, you can make it in a food processor. But don't make it absolutely smooth—a slightly chunky texture is ideal.

Mayonnaise

Homemade mayonnaise is surprisingly easy to make, especially in a food processor. Making it yourself lets you subtly vary the taste by using more or less flavorful oils. You can also add your favorite herbs to make a distinctive mayonnaise to accent sandwiches. Basil, parsley, tarragon, chervil, and thyme all work well.

Makes 1½ cups

  2 **egg yolks**
¼ **teaspoon prepared mustard**
¼ **teaspoon salt**
     Pinch of white pepper
1¼ **cups oil (see Note)**
  3 **tablespoons lemon juice or white vinegar**

1. Have all the ingredients at room temperature. Place the egg yolks, mustard, salt, and pepper in the food processor work bowl. Process until pale yellow and foamy. Add a tablespoonful of oil and mix until it is absorbed. If your feed tube has a small hole in it, pour the rest of the oil through the tube; it will drip through at just the right speed. If your tube doesn't have a hole, dribble the oil in very slowly until the mixture thickens. Continue adding oil until half of it has been used, then start alternating small amounts of oil and lemon juice or vinegar. (You can simply add the lemon juice or vinegar to the oil in the feed tube; it will sink through the oil and dribble in through the hole.) Continue until all the oil has been incorporated. The mayonnaise will be yellower than commercial mayonnaise.

2. Taste the mayonnaise, and correct the seasoning if necessary. Store tightly covered in the refrigerator. Homemade mayonnaise will keep for a week or more. White patches may appear on the surface after a few days; these are caused by some of the moisture separating, and are not a sign of spoilage. Scrape them off if they bother you.

NOTE For the plainest taste, use a neutral-tasting vegetable oil such as safflower or peanut. I like to use about half olive oil (an everyday oil, not extra-virgin; see page 12) for a fuller flavor.

VARIATION To make mayonnaise with an electric mixer or a whisk, warm a stainless steel or glass mixing bowl with warm water and wipe it dry. Combine the egg yolks and seasonings as above and beat until pale yellow and foamy. Twist a kitchen towel into a circle and set the bowl in it to keep it steady. Beat with one hand as you pour in the oil with the other. Incorporate the oil and vinegar in the same sequence as above.

Fresh Tomato Salsa

This salsa is used mainly in the Mexican recipes in this book, but there's no reason you can't use it on a roast beef, ham, or turkey sandwich.

Makes 1 cup

1 large tomato, peeled, seeded, and finely diced
1 green onion, minced
1 small green chile such as serrano or jalapeño, seeds and ribs removed, minced
2 tablespoons chopped fresh coriander (cilantro) (optional)
Salt and lemon or lime juice to taste

Combine all the ingredients and let them stand 15 minutes to allow the flavors to blend. Taste for seasoning and correct if necessary. For the best texture and flavor, use the salsa on the day you make it. For a hotter flavor, chop the whole chile—seeds, ribs, and all.

Dried Chile Salsa

Each kind of dried chile, from the large *ancho, mulato,* New Mexico, and California varieties to the smaller, hotter *cascabel, árbol,* and *serrano seco,* will give its own flavor to this sauce. With any chile, removing the seeds and ribs makes a milder sauce; including them makes it hotter.

Makes ½ cup

2 large dried chiles or 1 ounce smaller chiles
1 small clove garlic
¼ cup water
Salt to taste

Heat a griddle or skillet and toast the chiles on the ungreased surface until they are pliable and fragrant; do not let them get too dark. Let them cool until they begin to get brittle, then tear or slit them open and remove as much of the seeds and ribs as desired. Tear the chiles into pieces and put them in a blender or food processor. Toast and peel the garlic and add it to the blender. Add the water and a pinch of salt, let the mixture stand 10 minutes, and blend to a slightly chunky consistency. Taste for salt and add more if necessary. The sauce will keep in the refrigerator for a week or more.

Clockwise from left: Almond Butter, Herbed Mustard, Fresh Tomato Salsa, Hot Brown Mustard, Tapenade

Homemade Mustard

If you want to experiment with your own mustard blends, all you need are a couple of varieties of whole mustard seeds from a spice shop and a spice grinder. Here are two recipes to get you started.

For the hottest mustards, mix the mustard seeds with cold liquids, which preserve all the pungent volatile oils in the seeds. Mixing a boiling hot liquid with the ground seeds and stirring the mixture over low heat releases a lot of the oils (as your nose and sinuses will immediately tell you), resulting in a milder, smoother mustard.

I recommend that you work with whole seeds and grind them just before mixing. Even the best powdered mustards change with time and exposure to air, resulting in a harsher, dustier flavor. An electric coffee grinder with rotating blades is ideal for grinding spices thoroughly and quickly. If using the same one you use for coffee, grind a tablespoonful of raw rice before and after grinding spices to keep coffee and spices from flavoring one another.

Herbed Mustard

Slightly darker and grainier than a Dijon mustard, this is a good basic mustard for sandwiches. You can vary the herbs according to taste; don't blend too many, however, or the taste will become muddled. Try dill all by itself. Use about half as much dried herbs as fresh, but don't bother with dried chervil—it has absolutely no taste. And be sure to use a wine vinegar with character; some are amazingly insipid.

Makes ¾ cup

- ¼ cup yellow mustard seeds
- 1 tablespoon brown mustard seeds
- ¾ cup boiling water
- 1 to 2 teaspoons minced fresh herbs—tarragon, chervil, chives, or a combination
- ½ teaspoon salt
- 2 to 2½ tablespoons full-flavored wine vinegar

1. Grind the mustard seeds to a fine powder and place them in the top of a double boiler over simmering water. Add the boiling water to the seeds and stir the mixture well. Cook 15 minutes, keeping the water in the bottom of the double boiler at a lively simmer. Stir the mixture frequently, scraping down the sides of the pan with a rubber spatula; it will become a thick paste.

2. Remove the insert from the double boiler, stir to cool the mixture slightly, and stir in the herbs and salt. Add vinegar to taste, starting with 2 tablespoons and adding more if necessary. Let the mustard cool, transfer it to a jar, and seal it tightly. Age the mustard for a few days to a few weeks for better flavor.

Hot Brown Mustard

A higher proportion of brown mustard seeds and cold mixing make this a dark, pungent mustard. If you like a coarser texture, grind the seeds in a mortar rather than in the grinder, stopping when some whole and some cracked seeds remain.

Makes ½ cup

2 tablespoons each yellow and brown mustard seeds
1 tablespoon vinegar
2 tablespoons cold water
¼ teaspoon salt, or to taste

Grind the seeds together in a spice grinder or mortar. Combine all the ingredients in a small bowl and mix to a paste, adding a little more water or vinegar if needed. Cover and let stand overnight before serving.

INDEX